MORALITY of the HEART

A Psychology for the Christian Moral Life

CHARLES M. SHELTON

CROSSROAD • NEW YORK

1990

The Crossroad Publishing Company
370 Lexington Avenue, New York, NY 10017

Copyright © 1990 by Charles M. Shelton

Printed in the United States of America

Library of Congress Cataloging-in-Publication Data

Shelton, Charles M.
    Morality of the heart : a psychology for the Christian moral life
/ Charles M. Shelton.
      p.   cm.
    Includes bibliographical references.
    ISBN 0-8245-1052-6
    1. Christian ethics—Catholic authors. 2. Christianity—
Psychology 3. Empathy—Religious aspects—Christianity.
I. Title
BJ1249.S44   1990
241'.01'9—dc20   90-34748
                                              CIP

For Mom and Dad,
Lois, Phil, and Martha,
whose lives have taught
me the true meaning of the heart

Contents

Acknowledgements

This work would not be possible without the dedicated scholarship and pioneering efforts of several psychologists, notably: Lawrence Kohlberg, Norma Haan, and Carol Gilligan. Most of all, I am deeply indebted to the groundbreaking work of Martin Hoffman. His insights and writing in the field of developmental psychology, and in particular his emphasis on the development of empathy, have fascinated me while being an invaluable resource for shaping my own attempts to create a dialogue between theology and developmental theory. I also wish to express my deep appreciation and gratitude to Professor Dan P. McAdams. More than anything, Dan's belief in me as a psychologist has made my study of psychology an adventure as well as an on-going pleasure. Finally, I wish to express my appreciation to four dear friends who have been a constant support during the writing of this work: Jim Goggins, Jim Harbaugh, Harry Hoewischer, and John Ridgway. Their friendship this past year has proven invaluable.

≻ Chapter 1 ≺

Reconsidering Morality:
A Personal Perspective

In 1975 I was completing my master's degree and at the same time living in a college residence hall as a dormitory counselor. This living situation provided numerous opportunities for discussions with undergraduates. While conversing with them I became intrigued by a phenomenon I perceived in many students. A good number of these young adults were capable of penetrating and insightful understandings regarding their own personal relationships and the effects their behaviors had on their peers. On the other hand, I noticed that some students experienced difficulties in their own personal lives, hardships that often arose from their own lack of self-insight or their own misunderstanding of their friends' or others' feelings. Moreover, through conversations I noted that late adolescents' interests concerning moral questions about personal behaviors were closely linked to developmental issues. Most significant, moral concerns of youth were usually tied to relational themes. Questions of how one treats others and the need to have an accurate understanding of the other's thoughts and feelings were often paramount. Accordingly, I began to accept the view that some level of empathic experience was indispensable for experiencing oneself as a moral person and living the moral life.

Being actively engaged in ministry, I was naturally attracted to discussions of morality and variously related issues. I began to ask myself what it was about being *human* that allowed us to care for and be concerned with one another? Indeed, what human capacity fostered such care? The Christian response was, naturally, "love." Yet, more specifically, what is it about being human that allows us to love? Or, from another perspective, what is the constitutive element within our own human experience that, transformed by grace, allows us to

1

respond to the message of Jesus? If such an experience can be identified, then it seemed that helpful insights could be gathered about the
Christian's call to respond to Jesus' message (Mark 10:21). In essence,
the discipleship of Jesus must be rooted in our humanity — who we
are as humans. It is through our humanity that grace works its will
and beckons us forth. The action of grace seeks to transform our very
selves into a "wholly new realm of life, one in which the body is completely vivified by the grace of the Spirit" (Rom. 8:11). Thus, if this
aspect of our humanity can be addressed, then essential insights into
the Christian message can be offered.

These early thoughts stayed with me as I pursued my training in
the Jesuit order. Upon the completion of my master's work, I was
assigned for three years as an instructor in social science and a counselor at a Jesuit secondary school. I brought to this work my interests
in counseling and moral development. What I observed was that high
school youth, at a more elementary level than their college counterparts, shared the same developmental issues. Relationships with
family and friends often seemed the defining features of their identity.

One incident in particular proved a catalyst both for my thinking and for framing my future interest. I was teaching a course in
sociology to seniors. One day the class engaged in a lively discussion regarding social class and upward mobility. One senior (I will
call him Tom) made a rather forceful argument for the idea that
a person could achieve and become anything he or she wanted to.
The only thing standing in a person's way was his or her motivation
to achieve. In contrast to Tom's argument for rugged individualism,
another student, Jim, disagreed strongly. Jim maintained that one
could not necessarily achieve simply because one wanted to. On the
contrary, he pointed out that there existed many sources of discrimi-
nation and obstacles in our society that often prevented people from
pursuing what they desired to become.

Interestingly, the backgrounds of these students were revealing.
Tom's background was upper middle class. His father was a successful businessman and Tom had been given many opportunities over
the years. Jim's background, in contrast, was quite different. He came
from a lower-class family and his father was periodically unemployed.
The point I wish to make, of course, is how the background of each
student shaped his current views. Jim had seen (and experienced) numerous obstacles to achievement. In other words, he had empathized
with the suffering and insecurities of others (members of his family
and those in his neighborhood). Tom, on the other hand, had not
experienced such obstacles. His life had been shielded from the suf-

ferings Jim endured, thereby giving him only limited opportunities to empathize with others' plight. It was not that Tom lacked compassion or sensitivity; indeed, I knew him to be a very sensitive and caring adolescent. Yet he had not had the experiences that allowed him to empathize to the degree that Jim had.

As I thought later about this class discussion, I came to realize that "empathy" was the key that unlocked the capacity for caring for others. Without the experience of empathy it would be virtually impossible effectively to instruct students about the Christian message. For me, this insight proved a catalyst for later academic pursuits. I began to read avidly in the areas of psychology in general, and moral development in particular. The writings of Lawrence Kohlberg began to occupy my time. Yet while I was reading I sensed a growing discontent with the framework in which psychology, particularly the cognitive-developmental approach of Kohlberg, interpreted morality. I found it difficult to reconcile Kohlberg's view with people's everyday human experience. In other words, one's personal experience of being moral was at variance with the moral psychology offered by Kohlberg. My own observations of and interactions with others led me to conclude that another approach was necessary. A view of morality was needed that dealt with human experience as expressed in current psychological theory and that both addressed the ordinary cares and concerns of everyday life and was at the same time compatible with the Christian message. I have great sympathy with Paul Tillich's remark that "morality for ordinary people is not the result of reading books and writing papers, as we're doing. Morality is not a *subject*; it is a life put to the test in dozens of moments."[1] Discussions of morality must address the human experience that interacts with these everyday "tests."

It is my belief (indeed, the theme of this book) that this moral experience is rooted in the human capacity for empathy and that this capacity forms the human foundation to accept the Gospel's command to love. Over the last few years my own work in moral development has been to stress the essential importance of an affective component for any theory of moral development.[2] In essence, for a morality to be truly Christian, it must also be truly human. In other words, it must incorporate along with its transcendent dimension the reality of human experience.

Jerome Kagan has observed:

Construction of a persuasive rational basis for behaving morally has been the problem on which most moral philosophers have stubbed their toes. I believe they will continue to do so until they recognize what Chinese philosophers have appreciated for a long time: namely, feeling, not logic, sustains the superego.[3]

The human experience that resonates most readily with these "feelings" is empathy. In both my clinical and pastoral work, I have come to see that an individual's defining of self as moral has as much if not more to do with an innate sense of bonding and attachment as it does with defining what is just (which is Kohlberg's emphasis).

One need not reflect long to realize the profound import of empathy for our moral lives. A child who becomes a parent and bears the joys, trials, and tribulations of parenting soon grows to develop a deepening appreciation for his or her own parents. The psychologist who suffers a family death develops a deepening sensitivity for the psychological effects of any loss that a client experiences. A sociology professor who spends several days riding with police officers becomes sensitized to the fears and frustrations that they encounter and realizes the demanding nature of the officer's job. A legislator whose family has a handicapped child develops a different view of and deepening appreciation for legislation that provides educational funding for the handicapped. A reader whose own life has been marked by suffering can more readily identify with the portrayal that a writer attempts to create in her characters. In all these cases and countless more, one comes to realize that such empathic experiences are bound to shape one's experience as a moral person as well as the interpretation one gives moral issues. Of equal importance, arising out of these experiences is a deepening appreciation for and sensitivity to the struggles and problems that people undergo. From attention given to our empathic yearnings, we most often become more understanding and caring — the *heart* of the Gospel message.

Any serious discussion of morality is bound to be complex. Moreover, even attempting a definition of morality invites controversy and debate. The intricate nature of morality's meaning suggests the need for an interdisciplinary approach; moreover, there are many ways to view morality, each with their own advantages (as well as disadvantages). One is ill-advised to adopt any one discipline's view of morality without attending to the insights provided by other subject matter. More to the point, to discuss morality seriously means to enlist the disciplines of theology, philosophy, and education as well as the social sciences, particularly psychology, in an interdisciplinary dialogue. At the same time, any writer naturally speaks within the context of his or her own training and field of study. My training is in psychology and it is this perspective that I bring to any moral discussion, specifically, the emphasis on *human experience*. In making this statement I am aware of psychologists' tendency to commit the "empirical fallacy" — that is, the mistaken assumption that all of truth is obtained through observable behavior. On the contrary, people continuously give meanings to their behavior by attending to the workings of internal processes (e.g., dreams, hopes, ideals).[4] Peoples' aspirations and desire for an ideal morality occupy a powerful motivating force in the human psyche. Even so, the pages that follow do not offer some idealized view of morality, which at times can be the pitfall of theological speculation. Instead, I hope to address the powerful capacity within each of us that orients our moral quest toward loving care (not of course that it is always acted upon).

Educators Donald Oliver and Mary Jane Bane note that "educators, philosophers, and psychologists should join with theologians and sensitive youth in a search for the kind of powerful metaphor with which our Christian heritage once provided us."[5] If we attend closely to human experience I believe that such a metaphor is readily available. By proposing the "heart" as the basic metaphor for Christian morality, I hope to be true both to human experience and the continuing challenge of the Gospel message. Only through such interdisciplinary dialogue can we come to realize that the "message of truth, the Gospel" can and does bear "fruit." Moreover, from an examination of a heart morality, we come to see that, indeed, it is possible that the message of Christ will continue "to grow in your midst, as it has everywhere in the world" (Col. 1:6).

> Chapter 2 <

The Kohlberg Legacy

Questions regarding the meaning of morality have always been an essential focus for human inquiry. Indeed, the very functioning and continuity of human societies requires discussion of morality's nature. "Although the specific definitions may vary, there is an acknowledgment that morality constitutes the basic fabric of societal and interpersonal relations."[1] Though there exists near universal agreement about morality's indispensability, a breakdown of this consensus quickly ensues when the question surfaces as to what constitutes morality's essential elements.

Moreover, psychologists note that humans possess an "unremitting need" to view themselves as moral persons. According to traditional psychoanalytic theory, the nature of defense mechanisms originates in the psyche's need to protect itself from the stark truth of its own fallibility. "Freud's theory of the ego defenses depends on the single observation that humans will resort to all means of self-deception to fortify their view of themselves as moral."[2]

The importance of morality for people's lives has not gone unnoticed in social science circles. In addition to the domains of theology and philosophy, the last two decades have spawned a rich and provocative array of psychological observations on moral thinking. In fact, the study of morality has become a true interdisciplinary effort incorporating not only the traditional humanities but the works of psychologists, educators, sociologists, and biologists. Writing on this very topic, social psychologist Norma Haan has observed that "issues concerning moral meanings in people's lives can not be ignored if social science is to be complete and competent."[3]

In the pages that follow we accept as a premise the need for a multi-faceted approach to morality. Nonetheless, this perspective is decidedly psychological. More importantly, set forth in these pages is

6

a psychological view of morality that establishes the unity of human experience with the Christian moral vision. In other words, I propose that, based on psychological research, we can conclude that *our humanity is oriented to receive the offer of God's self-communicating presence and be transformed so as to fulfill more completely the command to love* (John 15:17).

In order to present a psychological view of morality consonant with the Christian moral vision, we must first explore what psychologists have been saying about morality. In this regard, attention must first be given to the work of Lawrence Kohlberg. Indeed, discussion of the psychological meaning of morality can only proceed from an understanding of both the merits and inadequacies of Kohlberg's approach. His significance for a psychology of morality arises for two reasons. First, Kohlberg has provided to date the most theoretically integrated and empirically tested theory of morality. Thus, psychological investigations of morality must consider his approach before offering alternatives. Secondly, Kohlberg's moral theory, among all psychological theories of morality, enjoys support in educational, philosophical, and theological circles. For example, it is estimated that over five thousand school districts have utilized aspects of Kohlberg's theory in their curricula. Millions of students have been exposed in one way or another (e.g., through teaching methods, class discussion) to his ideas.[4]

The Background for Kohlberg's Theory

Kohlberg's theory can best be understood through a contrast with attempts by educators to develop some understanding of the relationship of values and moral behavior. The two principal movements in this area were the values education movement of the 1960s and the character trait studies undertaken by Hartshorne and May in the 1920s. Kohlberg viewed both of these movements as failed attempts to develop a viable and universal moral theory. The failed attempts of these two approaches served as a catalyst for his own efforts.

The value clarification approach objected to moralizing in the classroom and advocated student participation as a way to foster the development of the child or adolescent's personal value system. In other words, this approach attempts to develop the student's recognition of specific values and an awareness as to how these personal values are reflected in the child's behavior. Essentially, this approach encourages students — through a method of value processing — to prize, to choose, and to act on values they deem appropriate for a given situation. The inadequacy of values clarification approaches, says Kohlberg, resides in the relativity to which all values are reduced. As a consequence, any and all values are options for students. Kohlberg has pointed out that a value clarification approach, in order to be consistent, must even allow cheating to be a legitimately chosen option for the student. The crux of Kohlberg's argument against this approach resides in his belief that values clarification methods lack a moral reference point; in other words, there exists no criterion by which to evaluate values, thereby leading to a moral hodge podge that lacks clarity.

Equally important, Kohlberg presented a strong attack upon the character studies that were popular through the earlier part of the twentieth century. In the 1920s Hartshorne and May embarked upon a massive character study of over ten thousand elementary and secondary school students. These researchers employed over thirty behavioral tests to measure behaviors associated with a "virtuous" character. Having surveyed religious leaders and educators, Hartshorne and May constructed an agreed upon list of behaviors that virtuous children and adolescents would carry out (e.g., altruistic acts, instances of self-control). In addition to these tests, teachers rated students on lists of virtuous characteristics. However, the results of these tests proved disappointing; the relationships resulting from these tests were generally low. These findings led Hartshorne and May to conclude that positive behaviors such as altruistic acts were "situation specific." That is, these researchers found no evidence of a "moral character" that directed one's behavior across a variety of situations. On the contrary, their findings led to the conclusion that behaviors were largely dependent on the situation at hand. Students might act honestly in one situation and dishonestly in another setting. Little evidence was found for a consistent moral character or general moral traits. The inevitable conclusion of these findings was that a consistent moral character was not substantiated. When commenting upon these disappointing results, Kohlberg has noted that "it is a fair statement of the history of psychological research in the field to say that the study of character as a set of virtues has not been a flourishing or successful research paradigm."[5] As a general comment, Kohlberg characterized the Hartshorne and May studies as exemplifying a "bag of virtues" approach to morality. Moreover, Kohlberg believed that the behaviors listed by the Hartshorne and May studies as "virtuous" were in fact culturally relative. Not only did people behave differently in various situations, but the behaviors themselves were subject to different interpretations by various groups and cultures. An inescapable conclusion drawn from these findings was that morality would be viewed as relative. Kohlberg's own efforts have been a direct challenge to such cultural relativism.

In contrast to an approach that focuses on the behavioral study of traditionally accepted positive behaviors, Kohlberg insisted that there exists an "internal component" involved in moral action. This point is crucial in understanding the essential thrust of Kohlberg's theory. Whereas morality is usually viewed as associated with "behavior" (e.g., the actions studied in the previously mentioned character studies), Kohlberg stresses one's understanding of moral experience as the cornerstone of morality. That is, what is essential in explaining morality is an internal frame of reference, which for Kohlberg is moral reasoning, or the emphasis on rational reflection. Throughout his nearly thirty years of research, Kohlberg maintained that there exists a "universal ontogenetic trend toward the development of morality"[6] as it has been set forth by Western moral philosophers. In effect, Kohlberg's writings underscore his acceptance of what is known as a deontological ethical position. Essentially, this position argues that morality is based on principles universally binding on all human beings regardless of the consequences. In other words, all reasonable human beings, regardless of culture, could reason to the same conclusion as to the validity of some ethical positions.

Kohlberg states that his focus

on morality as deontological justice springs, in part, from a concern with moral and ethical universality in moral judgment. The search for moral universality implies the search for some minimal value conception(s) on which all persons could agree, regardless of personal differences in detailed aims or goals.[7]

The "method" Kohlberg utilizes in his theory is calculated through responses that subjects give to dilemmas (a story in which a protagonist is faced with an ethical decision that usually involves the breaking of some rule). The most famous of these dilemmas is the "Heinz dilemma" in which Heinz is faced with the difficult situation of deciding whether he should steal a drug to save the life of his wife who is desperately ill. The druggist refuses to bring down the price to make the drug affordable and Heinz is confronted with the reality of either stealing the drug and breaking the law or allowing his wife to die. Heinz decides to steal the drug. Through a complex scoring system, Kohlberg scores the "reasons" the subject gives for deciding whether Heinz should or should not steal the drug. This analysis of a subject's reasons allows him or her to be placed at a particular stage.

Kohlberg has set forth a three-level–six-stage theory of morality that is invariant (there is no deviation from the stages as they are set forth), sequential (individuals must pass through the previous stage before arriving at a higher stage), hierarchical (higher stages are capable of taking into account lower-stage thinking while at the same time dealing with more complex issues and problems), and cross-cultural (Kohlberg's studies have found that people in other countries respond in similar orderly sequences to the dilemmas). Individuals tend to prefer the highest stage in which they can reason; these stages have been empirically validated in longitudinal studies by Kohlberg and his associates.

According to Kohlberg, the central, underlying principle that forms the basis for morality is the individual's understanding of justice. Kohlberg has stated that "there is a natural sense of justice intuitively known by the child."[8] Accordingly, an individual reasons about values, life dilemmas, and personal choices in the context of an understanding of justice that is appropriate for his or her own stage. Kohlberg firmly places himself within the cognitive-developmental tradition of Piaget. That is, a cognitive-developmental theory of moral development accepts a sequential order of moral stages for the same reason that there are cognitive stages: one's interaction with the environment leads to a *reorganization* of mental structures that are more capable of dealing with various dilemmas, life problems, and complex situations.

To explain briefly, the cognitive-developmental view, as represented in Piaget's theory of cognitive development, maintains that ongoing maturation and interaction with the environment lead to advancement in cognitive growth. At the sensorimotor level (ages zero to two) cognition is limited to experiences of the senses and action. From ages two to seven cognition is represented through images and words; however, the child's cognitive powers are without logical thought. Thus, the child engages in fantasy, takes statements literally, and incessantly asks "why" questions in order to develop a deepening understanding of his or her surroundings. Around the age of seven the child begins to acquire logical understanding. As a consequence, the child can now do basic arithmetic operations such as addition, subtraction, etc. Yet this use of logic is limited to concrete events. It is only with the advent of formal thinking at around the age of twelve that the child acquires the capacity for abstraction, deepening reflection, hypothesis building. It is in adolescence that one begins to think more reflectively, to wonder about various possibilities, and to acquire the critical thinking that questions and challenges adult ways of thinking. For example, if the child in concrete thinking is asked what would it be like if he or she did not exist, the answers would be limited to very factual ones such as "there would only be four people in my family instead of five," "twenty-nine people in my class instead of thirty." On the other hand, an adolescent's response would move beyond such concrete facts. He or she could speak of missed opportunities, of the effects on others, of the future and the loss of what might have been.[9]

The three levels and six stages that make up Kohlberg's theory are set forth below. Admirably, Kohlberg has responded to critical comments and challenges to his theory over the years through some significant revisions. Commentators, however, have found these revisions to be bewildering. As Richard Shweder notes, "It is complex enough to dazzle even the most sympathetic critic."[10] The most common understanding of his theory is the traditional formula reproduced below. I will make reference to various revisions of his theory when appropriate in order to point out the changes as well as Kohlberg's attempts to "hear" the numerous reactions and criticisms his theory have stimulated.

I. Preconventional Level

At this level, the child is responsive to cultural rules and labels of good and bad, right or wrong, but interprets these labels either in terms of the physical or hedonistic consequences of action (punishment, reward, exchange of favors) or in terms of the physical power of those who enunciate the rules and labels. The level is divided into the following two stages:

Stage 1: The punishment-and-obedience orientation. The physical consequences of action determine its goodness or badness, regardless of the human meaning or value of these consequences.

Stage 2: The instrumental-relativist orientation. Right action consists of that which instrumentally satisfies one's own needs and occasionally the needs of others.

II. Conventional Level

At this level, maintaining the expectations of the individual's family, group, or nation is perceived as valuable in its own right, regardless of immediate and obvious consequences. The attitude is not only one of conformity to personal expectations and social order, but of loyalty to it, of actively maintaining, supporting, and justifying the order, and of identifying with the persons or group involved in it. At this level, there are the following two stages:

Stage 3: The interpersonal concordance or "good boy-nice girl" orientation. Good behavior is that which pleases or helps others and is approved by them. There is much conformity to stereotypical images of what is majority or "natural" behavior.

Stage 4: The "law and order" orientation. There is orientation toward authority, fixed rules, and the maintenance of the social order. Right behavior consists of doing one's duty, showing respect for authority, and maintaining the given social order for its own sake.

III. Postconventional, autonomous, or principled level

At this level, there is a clear effort to define moral values and principles that have validity and application apart from the authority of the groups or persons holding these principles and apart from the individual's own identification with these groups. This level also has two stages:

Stage 5: The social-contract, legalistic orientation, generally with utilitarian overtones. Right action tends to be defined in terms of general individual rights and standards that have been critically examined and agreed upon by the whole society. There is a clear awareness of the relativism of personal values and opinions and a corresponding emphasis upon procedural rules for reaching consensus.

Stage 6: The universal-ethical-principle orientation. Right is defined by the decision of conscience in accord with self-chosen ethical principles appealing to logical comprehensiveness, universality, and consistency. These principles are abstract and ethical (the Golden Rule, the categorical imperative); they are not concrete moral rules like the Ten Commandments. At heart, these are universal principles of justice, of the reciprocity and equality of human rights, and of respect for the dignity of human beings as individual persons.[11]

A reading of the stages above leads one to conclude there exists a distinctive theme for each level. The preconventional level is decidedly egotistic. Reasoning at this stage is directed by one's need for reward and punishment and the desire for pleasure. A distinctive feature of this stage is the self-centered nature of moral reasoning. Rarely, according to Kohlberg, does one take into consideration the needs of others. On the contrary, the deciding references for one's thinking are self-centered rationales that enhance one's own standing or situation. These reasoning levels are most often contained in the thinking patterns of children who are unable to abstract from the self to the needs and concerns of others.

In contrast to the preconventional level's narrowing focus on the self, the conventional level admits to a widening perspective that incorporates the needs and concerns of others. For example, at stage 3, there is the realization of other people's perceptions and the need to consider their expectations. An even more expanded view of social relationships is found in stage 4, where appreciation is given to the rules and customs of society or the prevailing environment (e.g., civil law, the rules of the school, the tacit assumptions that guide the workings of the peer group). Kohlberg notes that the vast majority of people utilize reasoning associated with conventional moral thinking. Individuals commonly appeal to the rules and customs of their family, social groups, society, to explain and justify their behaviors. What is termed "just," in other words, is what authority figures or the law determines. What needs to be noted, though, is that there exists a decisive shift that incorporates attention to the views and thinking of others; as a consequence, justice is not solely determined by one's needs. Rather, the thinking and views of others are incorporated into one's reasoning about justice. At this level, justice is likely to resemble the customs, traditions, and rules that are reflected by society or significant groups to which one is attached (e.g., church, ethnic identity, or, for an adolescent, the peer group).

Kohlberg's belief in the moral supremacy of rational reflection is best captured by his emphasis on postconventional thinking, which, for Kohlberg, is the *essence* of the moral point of view. Reasoning at this level moves beyond conventions and finds its basis in abstract philosophical principles. No longer is one's reasoning about justice guided by convention; rather, there exists an appeal to moral principles that can be rationally construed and accepted by all rational persons, regardless of cultural background. In other words, when one utilizes postconventional thought, an individual is reflecting the moral principles of justice exemplified through respect for persons, equality, and individual rights, moral principles that Western philosophical traditions have accepted as legitimate.

According to Blum, the distinctive feature of Kohlberg's "justice morality" is the focus on impartiality:

there is one, unitary, distinct "moral point of view," which is impartial, universal, impersonal, objective, and rational. Morality takes the form of universal principles — principles applicable to all human beings — guiding the moral agent to right or obligatory action. To be moral the agent must abstract himself from his individual interests and particular relationships; he must adopt an impartial standpoint favoring no person over any other. Moral principles thus generated cannot be confined merely to the customs or mores of any particular society. They must at bottom rest on a rational and universal foundation that transcends the agent's own society (or *any* particular society, for that matter), though particular principles of his own society that can be validated from that perspective may be included in the set of morally acceptable action-specifying principles.[12]

For Kohlberg, each stage of moral reasoning is a "structured whole," or what might be termed a systematic organization of thought that reflects a unique understanding of justice for that particular stage. How an individual reasons about the dilemma defines the level of structure (stage) of the person. This is crucial for the understanding of Kohlberg's system, for his emphasis is on "how" one reasons, rather than on the content of the reasoning. For example, in the Heinz dilemma, the issue is not what one believes Heinz should do (what we term the "content" of the dilemma). The issue for the cognitive developmental view is how one reasons, which in turn is a reflection of one's structure of reasoning.

Kohlberg believes that moral growth, like cognitive development, allows for increasingly moral structural transformations. These transformations (movement to a higher stage) are the result of life experience, increasing capacity for role-taking (taking the perspective of another), encounters with and discussions about hypothetical dilemmas (a favorite classroom technique of the cognitive-developmentalists is to pose hypothetical dilemmas and encourage reflection and the awareness of higher-stage thinking that proves more adequate than one's own, thus the realization that there exists more adequate thinking beyond one's own moral reasoning), and most recently, the importance of the existence of a socio-moral environment that fosters the just community.[13]

As a consequence, given the foregoing experiences, an individual's reasoning enters a period of disequilibrium that invites stage advancement. "In essence, there is a 'deep logical structure' of movement from one stage to the next; a structure tapped by both a psychological theory of movement and by families of philosophical argument."[14] Moreover, each stage reflects a more adequate understanding of the justice principle because inherent in each stage of moral development is a greater degree of differentiation and integration. That is, each stage, because of its differentiated and integrating capacities is, in essence, a more mature structure capable of addressing the complexity and variability inherent in life dilemmas, conflicts, and differing points of view. Thus, higher stages are more adequate than lower stages because of their capacity for incorporating a variety of perspectives and dealing with the complex nature of the dilemma at hand.

Even so, though each stage underscores a distinctive understanding of the justice principle, it is only at stage 6 that justice embraces the attributes of fairness, equality, and reciprocity. Only at this stage does justice become universally acceptable because only stage 6 morality incorporates a view of justice that all rational persons regardless of cultural background or existential situation could agree upon.

A Critique of Kohlberg's Theory

As noted above, Kohlberg's theory has achieved enormous influence. I have argued elsewhere why I think his theory has obtained the ascendancy it has in religious and educational circles.[15] In brief, the breakdown in institutional codes and systematic ways of thinking and behaving (uncritically accepted as legitimate before the mid-sixties) led to a "vacuum" that educators and parents were at a loss to explain and even less capable of filling. The ensuing clash of views and the inherent conflicts led for a search as to an acceptable and coherent theory to explain moral behavior. The systematic, methodical, and empirically tested nature of Kohlberg's theory and his stress on "moral development" won ready acceptance, at least initially, from educators. Over time, however, there has developed a growing body of literature that is critical of Kohlberg's theory.[16]

In the pages that follow I offer a critique of his thinking with emphasis on those aspects of his theory that prove problematic for the Christian understanding of morality. In short, these criticisms can be placed under one of four categories.

The Question of a Sixth Stage

With the initial publication of his theory and throughout the early years of his research, Kohlberg optimistically spoke of the attainment of principled moral thinking. By the late seventies Kohlberg was less sanguine about achieving such a goal. What took place was a gradual "retrenchment." For example, the goal for adolescents became, simply, a grounding in conventional morality (stage 4). Movement to principled thinking (stage 5) necessitated a combination of life experiences, active, and ongoing questioning about life choices, commitment to personal decisions, and corresponding moral reflection. Says Kohlberg:

> In summary, personal experiences of choice involving questioning and commitment, in some sort of integration with stimulation of cognitive-moral reflection, seems required for movement from conventional to principled (Stage 5) thought. It is probably for this reason that principled thought is not attained in adolescence.[17]

More importantly, though, was Kohlberg's failure to validate a sixth stage of moral reasoning. When Kohlberg initially published his theory, a considerable degree of criticism focused on his methodology and scoring procedures for the various stages.[18] In response to his critics, Kohlberg revised his scoring system. However, a reanalysis of his data did not support the presence of a sixth stage.

Nonetheless, Kohlberg has reemphasized in his own theory the importance of truly principled morality (stage 6). Although no longer maintaining the empirical verifiability of stage 6, Kohlberg now views the theoretical possibility of a principled morality evinced in stage 6 thinking as of considerable import.

The present position of stage 6 thinking, moreover, appears to provide two features. First, justice has come to operate as a *functional* component inasmuch as it offers a conceptual understanding for his theory. Thus Kohlberg argues that "a terminal stage, with the principle of justice as its organizing principle, helps us to define the area of human activity under study."[19] Secondly, he appears to view stage 6, in the current sketch of his theory, as an "ideal end point" for the development of the more limited understandings of justice articulated at lower stages. Even so, the recent scoring revisions show only minimal support even for stage 5 thinking, the lower half of principled morality. Thus, one critic has noted that "stage 5 even in minor traces is a rarity"[20] and that, in general, movement from one stage to another is an exceedingly slow process wherein most change occurs among only a few stages (usually from two to four). In other words, growth in moral development appears centered on a small central area of the overall theory with scant movement at higher stages.

Nonetheless, Kohlberg hypothesizes the presence of a stage 7. Thinking at this stage is concerned with life issues and questions that go beyond the rational philosophic questions characteristic of his own stage theory. For example, questions such as "Why be a moral person?" "Why is there evil?" are the domain of this stage. In entertaining the idea of a stage 7, Kohlberg acknowledges the limitations of his theory to account for all meaningful life questions. In this respect, Kohlberg has appeared open and sensitive to his critics and has attempted to "hear" their concerns. "Generally speaking, a Stage 7 response to ethical and religious problems is based on constructing a sense of identity or unity with being, with life, or with God."[21] Thus, he associates stage 7 with more theistically based orientations. In sum, even though there is absent an empirically verifiable sixth stage, Kohlberg argues for its inclusion as an ideal end-point in an individual's on-going moral development.

What are we to make of Kohlberg's belief in principled morality (even with his inability to verify movement to principled morality)? As I read Kohlberg, I suspect his "heart" is with the development of principled morality and his desire is to find a universally valid moral theory, a desire that from his perspective would remain unrealized if he accepted other notions of morality (for example, love, an affective basis for morality). A glimpse of his own struggle to work out a moral theory is contained in his acceptance of a seventh stage and his willingness to "hear" the concerns of his critics about morality. On the other hand, Kohlberg still insists on the primacy of the justice principle. He notes:

> Morality as justice best renders our view of morality as universal. It restricts morality to a central minimal core, striving for universal agreement in the face of more relativist conceptions of the good.[22]

Given the above passage, it becomes clear that Kohlberg believes that it is the universality of justice — the principles that all rational people could agree upon, regardless of cultural upbringing and personal life situation — that sways him to endorse the rationally based justice orientation that is most exemplified by postconventional thinking. As I read Kohlberg I believe his great fear is that to consider other sources of morality as alternatives to the justice principle is, in essence, to undercut what for him is *the* true morality. That is, morality would then be relegated to multiple meanings, each dependent on cultural considerations, thereby making the very meaning of morality otiose.

Given the questionable nature of a sixth stage as well as the paucity of even the lesser stage 5 principled thinking, however, Kohlberg's view of morality is lacking in a very fundamental way. What does it mean to have a moral theory wherein the very essence of morality (justice reasoning at stage 6) is itself unobtainable? In the very ordinary demands of everyday life, the absence of principled thinking (the essence of true morality for Kohlberg) renders every man or woman compromised. An essential attribute of morality for everyday moral life must be its obtainability. This does not mean a person is consistently and always moral in every situation; sainthood, unfortunately, is a scarce commodity! The very fiber of our moral lives is rendered deficient, however, if we accept a view of the moral life that is, for all practical purposes, unreachable. Moreover, being a moral person must not only be an ideal we aspire to; it must also be obtainable to some degree.

Kohlberg writes as a psychologist, yet the philosophical threads woven throughout his theory qualify him as a philosopher. Certainly no psychologist has so systematically integrated philosophical ideas with empirical findings. Unfortunately, philosophers and theologians are prone to succumbing to the idealization error. The idealization error is, simply, that moral theorizing speaks of an ideal that too often the philosopher or theologian believes is obtainable. In effect, the idealization error leads theologians and philosophers to believe that their theoretical speculations are, in fact, obtainable. Their world is the ideal, which far too often ignores the stresses, conflicts, and compromises that touch all aspects of life. Social teachings, currently flowing forth from many Christian churches, at times fall victim to this error. Thus pronouncements regarding social justice positions must be sensitive to the realities of everyday life while at the same time challenging all to greater conversion. Moreover, the philosopher/theologian needs the findings of the social sciences in order to understand the normal everyday experiences of human functioning. Of course philosophers and theologians provide an indispensable role for psychologists, too. All too often psychologists can get mired in facts and data, thereby ignoring the ideals and cherished ideas that come to reflect the deepening core meanings that fashion an individual's moral life. I noted in chapter 1 the need for psychologists to be aware of the tendency to commit the empirical fallacy.

Controversy surrounds the study of morality because

> most scholars do not agree on a definition of morality. But psychologists may make a new and potentially important contribution; their research may provide fresh understandings about every person's practical morality that philosophers [and I would add here theologians] may have missed because of their detachment from life. At this time in the history of moral discussion, psychologists especially need to turn to philosophers [and I would add here theologians] to learn what might be, and philosophers [and theologians] especially need psychologists to learn what is.[23]

Kohlberg's view of morality as we look at his data leaves one in an almost intolerable position of desiring the moral, yet never really being able to obtain it.

The Relevance of Kohlberg's Theory for Everyday Moral Life

A second difficulty with Kohlberg's understanding of morality concerns the application of the justice principle to everyday life. Surprisingly, even though the concept of justice is the central focus for Kohlberg's moral system, the exact meaning that Kohlberg accords the justice principle is not always clear. He has defined justice as "equality," a moral principle, that is, "a mode of choosing" that all people will adopt in all situations, the resolution of competing claims, the "core of morality," "the agreement, contract, and impartiality of the law," and as an abstract formal principle containing characteristics termed by philosophical discourse as universality, inclusivity, consistency, and objectivity.

Regardless of the justice definition one adopts, the justice principle, when applied to Kohlberg's dilemmas, negotiates the conflicting rights and claims of individuals. As we have noted, morality for Kohlberg is focused on the resolution of these claims over a wide variety of dilemmas. From the standpoint of the nature of morality, however, interpreting morality as the resolution of rights and claims represents a narrowly circumscribed perspective. Furthermore, the emphasis on rights and duties underscores what many have believed to be the strong ideological bias in Kohlberg's system. Thus, as Gibbs and Schnell have observed, "Kohlbergian theory as currently constituted would indeed seem to be compromised by philosophical individualism with its ethnocentric and elitist ramifications and would appear to be in need of revision."[24] In other words, there exists a strong bias in Kohlberg's theory that champions philosophical liberalism that is most at home with academic discourse emphasizing rights and duties.

A second, more serious example of Kohlberg's narrow understanding of morality is that the dilemmas that Kohlberg utilizes to substantiate the empirical grounds for his theory limit moral context. In other words, individuals as moral agents frequently encounter moral situations far removed from the claims and rights that are so often resolved by appeals to rational discourse or abstract philosophical principles. More than anything, it is this reality that has led me to doubt the adequacy of Kohlberg's theory of morality. In both my clinical work and my pastoral work I have been with many people who have struggled over relationships, personal issues that touch the very core of moral identity, yet go far beyond questions of rights and duties. The hurt experienced in ruptured relationships, the inability to make a decision fraught with questionable consequences, or the stark reality of psychological pain lead to a wide variety of concerns and questions that are often removed from rational discourse, yet strike at the very core of how people come to know themselves as moral persons.

To support this point, studies have also questioned whether people actually are so rational and philosophical in their everyday moral decision making. When adolescents must face issues that center on their everyday concerns, they tend to reason at lower stages than when they answer questions about life and death issues involved in Kohlberg's hypothetical dilemmas.[25]

Why do individuals think differently when they are confronted in the practical everyday events of their lives with moral decisions and often reason at a lower moral stage? The answer to this question rests on one's personal investment in making decisions. Confronting a moral decision is not only a rational but an affective process as well. When people reason about practical and everyday decisions a part of themselves is invested in the decision that is fundamentally different from rational reflection. Moral dilemmas as proposed by Kohlberg, on the other hand, provide the luxury of being "safe" experiences. That is, since our ego is not invested in deciding about the rightness of the act (for example, how many of us would ever have to face the life and death dilemma that confronted Heinz), we can feel secure in proposing and stating lofty moral principles. Suppose, however, that the moral dilemma we confronted was something very real to our own life? To take several examples: How would we respond morally if the question focused on the need for ending a significant relationship in our lives? What would we do if as an administrator we had to write a letter of rebuke to a subordinate we were fond of? What would we say about a dilemma where, as a parent, we had to face our son or daughter's drug habit in a compassionate yet firm way? I seriously question whether Kohlberg's method addresses adequately these very human and yet so fundamentally moral questions. Yet it is questions such as these and their attending struggles that sculpt for us our self-definition of what it means to be moral. It is in attending to such struggles that the experience of our selves as moral persons unfolds. Such decisions, given the meaningfulness of the attachment and the self's attempt to create a sense of moral integrity, lead to a building of defenses that foster either moral perseverance or self-delusion. Moreover, the very significance of such relational experiences creates major stresses that also impact on the capacity to persevere morally.[26]

Kohlberg has acknowledged that an enlargement of the moral domain is a legitimate enterprise. At the same time, he appears resolute in the need for claiming justice as the basis for morality. For Kohlberg, justice is the only moral enterprise that can insure universality. Secondly, he believes that only justice is consonant with the rationalistic focus he champions. "This is true partly in the sense that justice asks for 'objective' or rational reasons and justifications for choice rather than being satisfied with subjective, 'decisionistic,' personal commitments to aims and to other persons."[27] The key word in this passage is "satisfied." I seriously doubt that Kohlberg can truly accept as equal other approaches to morality. In essence, for Kohlberg, conceptions of morality that are divorced from a justice basis are secondary; in some way they fail to measure up to the stringent standards that Kohlberg envisions necessary for morality. It is to Kohlberg's credit, though, that in his later writings he has focused on the need for the practical dimensions of living and has addressed the need for community-based environments such as school settings where individuals could share a sense of responsibility for everyday decisions.

The Tension Between an Ethics of Care and an Ethics of Justice

Essentially, the debate between an ethics of justice versus an ethics of care focuses on the nature of morality. As noted above, for Kohlberg, the essence of morality is found in the justice principle, which is applied impartially to competing claims or interests; in addition, this view of morality, or what Kohlberg terms "the moral point of view," is discovered through rational discourse. On the other hand, other researchers have preferred to view morality as an ethics of care.

Carol Gilligan is one of the major proponents of this point of view. Gilligan's thought is best exemplified in her provocative work, *In a Different Voice*. Gilligan's work results from three studies undertaken by her and her associates. The first study contained interviews of college sophomores and a follow-up study five years after graduation. The second study focused on women's experience of abortion and the reasoning utilized in making such a decision. A cross-sectional study of eight men and eight women at nine different ages was the focus of the third study; in addition, two men and two women were the subject of more intense interviews.

The results of these studies led Gilligan to claim the presence of a care orientation in women as opposed to the more rule-oriented morality of men. Borrowing upon recent revisions in psychoanalytic thinking, Gilligan weaves together a perspective of morality that values connectedness, interpersonal relationships, and a caring stance toward the needs of others. By contrast, she notes that the male view of morality is oriented toward separation, emphasis on the significance of rights and duties, and the need for just resolution of competing interests. Gilligan notes:

> The moral imperative that emerges repeatedly in interviews with women is an injunction to care, a responsibility to discern and alleviate the "real and recognizable trouble" of this world. For men, the moral imperative appears rather as an injunction to respect the rights of others and thus to protect from interference the rights to life and self-fulfillment.[28]

In addition to her claims of male-female orientations, Gilligan maintains that developmental theorists (e.g., Kohlberg) have unfairly advocated a male-oriented view of morality that, in effect, has undervalued the female moral orientation that prizes care and connectedness. In this respect, the female orientation has been unfairly viewed as simply a deviation from the male-oriented justice view of morality. In reality, men and women might use both "voices"; there is, however, a preference in females for a morality of care whereas for males the preference is a morality of justice. These two moral orientations transform morality in a way that neither could envision separately.[29]

A review of *In a Different Voice* noted that "this book [Gilligan's] has created an unusual excitement within and beyond the field of psychology, no doubt because it is full of exciting ideas."[30] Yet a close scrutiny raises questions, says some critics, as to the adequacy of Gilligan's claims. Studies that analyze differences between the sexes are mixed. There is some evidence that suggests male-female difference regarding some aspects of social behavior and occupational choice. Other areas of development, however, specifically cognitive maturation and aspects of personal behaviors, show no difference. "The available research data, therefore, do not reveal a clear picture of global dichotomy between the life orientation of men and women."[31] Even so, the fuzzy nature of much of the research does not undercut Gilligan's assertions.

Kohlberg also has argued against Gilligan's thesis. He readily acknowledges that his original findings were based solely on male subjects. He also accepts Gilligan's assertion that an ethics of care does indeed exist and maintains such a perspective "usefully enlarges the moral domain."[32] What he does challenge is Gilligan's claim that sex differences exist in moral reasoning. In fact, a large body of studies have shown that when one takes into account education and socioeconomic status, there exist no differences in moral reasoning scores obtained by men and women. Some reviewers have also questioned Gilligan's findings and report that "while her [Gilligan's] portrayal of general sex linked life orientations is intuitively appealing, the research evidence at this point does not support such a generalized distinction."[33]

For her part, Gilligan has presented further research supporting her claim to two orientations. Recently, she has theorized on the effect of early relational experiences as a foundational soil for the emergence of a care orientation.[34] Yet she acknowledges the need for both perspectives: "While it is true that either we are men or we are women and certain experiences may accrue more readily to one or the other sex, it is also true that the capacity for love and the appreciation of justice is not limited to either sex."[35] I am in sympathy with the thrust of Gilligan's work. Indeed, her thinking is a much needed counterbalance to Kohlberg. At the same time, one caution needing mention is the necessity of linking moral principles to a care orientation. In other words, is "care" enough? On what moral principles is a care orientation based? Would it not be all too easy to convince ourselves that we are caring when in fact what we have done is avoid a necessary challenge or confrontation that is integral to moral growth? If "love" is the basis for care, then what are the values or ethical norms that guide one's loving behavior? The place of moral principles needs further discussion in a care orientation.

From his vantage point, Kohlberg resolves the issue of an ethics of justice versus an ethics of care by interweaving these two perspectives into his own justice orientation. Kohlberg maintains that principled morality is concerned with the rights and duties of every person whereas a care orientation stresses the bondedness and connectedness one maintains with the entire community; in effect, both orientations champion mutual care and respect. In sum, Kohlberg credits Gilligan with enlarging "the moral domain beyond our focus on justice reasoning."[36] Nonetheless, he disallows her claim that there exist two moral orientations and prefers to view the justice orientations as conceptually adequate to accommodate an ethics of care.

Moreover, a critical reading of Kohlberg's reformulation shows that Kohlberg is attempting to acknowledge the importance of a care ethics, yet preserve the priority he assigns to the justice orientation. Accordingly, although Kohlberg argues that justice and care share a similar focus with respect to responsible concern toward humanity, a closer examination of the origin of justice in Kohlberg's theory reveals a distinctive bias toward a cognitive emphasis of morality thereby favoring the justice orientation. Thus the cognitive emphasis associated with moral reasoning, in effect, subordinates the more affect-laden response of care and benevolence to the cognitive view of justice.

In earlier writings, Kohlberg emphasized the need for "role-taking" (taking the perspective of another) in order to develop moral judgment. Yet throughout his writing there exist an appreciation and concern for the welfare of others that he views as inherent in the cognitive-developmental approach. Thus he writes that moral judgments entail "a concern for welfare consequences"[37] and that "the psychological unity of empathy and justice in moral role taking is also apparent at the very start of the moral enterprise."[38] Furthermore,

> Psychologically, both welfare concerns (role taking, empathy) and justice concerns, are present at the birth of morality and at every succeeding stage and take on more differentiated, integrated, and universalized forms at every step of development.[39]

And

> The centrality of role taking for moral judgment is based on sympathy for others, as well as in the notion that the moral judge must adopt the perspective of the "impartial spectator" or the "generalized other."[40]

In essence, Kohlberg views the sympathetic, emotionally laden empathic dimension as originating at the earliest stages of moral development. Even with this emphasis, however, he consistently views the cognitive dimension of role-taking as *the* means for advancing moral judgment and little mention is made of a more internal physical arousal to the plight of others (e.g., empathy) as a means for fostering stage development.

Using role-taking to advance moral development, however, is not quite as simple as Kohlberg would have us believe. For example, taking the perspective of another might in fact lead us to be resentful about another who has more resources or advantages than we do. As a consequence, what role-taking might serve to promote is not sensitivity but jealousy.[41] This crucial point cannot help but lead us to look elsewhere for a basis for morality or at least to consider other dimensions of morality beyond the cognitive.

In sum, Kohlberg appears in his writing to value an affect-laden basis for morality, yet his "heart" most certainly is with the cognitive dimension. To pose the question of an ethics of care, moreover, is to address a dimension of human experience beyond the cognitive. Care presupposes feelings, particularly those identified with compassion. We will explore this meaning later. What is essential now, however, is simply to note the narrowness of Kohlberg's theory and its basic inability to incorporate an emotional dimension to morality.

Social psychologist Norma Haan argues cogently that emotions are integral to any moral understanding. Whereas Kohlberg would view a moral problem in terms of the moral agent's dispassionate rise above contradictions and emotional turmoil, Haan would maintain that emotion is vital to the moral dialogue. In fact, a moral solution would be incomplete if it failed to consider the affective dimension.

> Emotions accompany and enrich understandings, and they convey far more authentic information about a person's position in a dispute than any well-articulated thoughts. In ordinary circumstances, emotions instruct and energize action. In situations of great moral costs, emotions can overwhelm and disorganize cognitive evaluations.[42]

Relatedly, as noted in our previous criticism of Kohlberg, emotions are apt to play a crucial role in the development of ego-defensiveness. In other words, everyday life situations that present moral difficulties for an individual are likely to evoke a variety of affective responses that are proportional to the situational meanings such encounters hold for the individual; in contrast, Kohlberg's hypothetical dilemmas are far removed from ego concerns and thereby enlist little personal investment.

Whether a subject is able to apply his or her moral competence to a real-life context seems not only to be a structural problem but rather a problem of affectively dealing with personal needs and self-interests in a situation.[43]

Moreover, it is arguable that it is this affective dimension that prevents individuals from obtaining higher levels of moral reasoning on Kohlberg's scale. Conventional morality (recall that this is a morality that adopts the view of the culture, the group, or significant others) offers security for interpreting one's world. To advance to postconventional thinking, in all likelihood, would create a significant amount of tension and anxiety and require in turn a large degree of psychic energy and commitment. In the everyday experience of life, individuals are more in need of accessible frames of reference that are comforting and that in turn provide some grounding and certitude for everyday life decisions, decision making for which they lack the time or intellectual sophistication to defend or justify in the midst of daily encounters.

Kohlberg's concern for considering the role of emotion is readily apparent from his own writing. He views emotions as "part" of moral development yet emotions "do not tell us anything directly about the specifically moral development of the subject."[44] All in all, Kohlberg is unable to maintain even an uneasy truce between cognition and affect. In essence, Kohlberg's position endorses the primacy of cognition.

Relegating emotion to a secondary status in moral development, however, is clearly at variance with the historical traditions of many ethical and religious approaches to morality that note that emotion exercises a critical role in human moral experience. The experience of conversion is a prime example of this broader perspective. Further, psychological circles have refocused thinking on the role of emotions. As we will point out later, this focus centers on the experience of empathy and the presence of early moral emotions.

The Question of Value Content

The final question regarding Kohlberg's theory is associated with the absence of a value content for moral development. As noted previously, Kohlberg's moral theory arose in part from his disillusionment with the "bag of virtues" approach. In the sixties Kohlberg disassociated his own theory from a content-laden approach that advocates distinct values and ethical guidelines. "In my view a culturally universal definition of morality can be arrived at if morality is thought of as the form of moral judgments instead of the content of specific moral beliefs."[45]

Kohlberg later altered his thinking on the nature of content for moral development. After working in several experimental educational settings, Kohlberg changed his absolute prohibition of value content and admitted the necessity of some content acquisition by students, though the adoption of values should arise from mutual dialogue among faculty, staff, and students.

> I realize now that the psychologist's abstraction of moral "cognition" (judgment and reasoning) from moral action, and the abstraction of structure in moral cognition and judgment from content are necessary abstractions for certain psychological research purposes. It is not a sufficient guide to the moral educator who deals with the moral concrete in a school world in which value content as well as structure, behavior as well as reasoning must be dealt with. In this context, the educator must be a socializer teaching value content and behavior, and not only a Socratic or Rogerian process-facilitator of development.[46]

Kohlberg goes on to state that

> I no longer hold these negative views of indoctrinative moral education and I believe that the concepts guiding moral education must be partly "indoctrinative." This is true, by necessity, in a world in which children engage in stealing, cheating, and aggression and in a context wherein one cannot wait until children reach the fifth stage to deal directly with moral behavior.[47]

Kohlberg's admission of the need for some prescribed values is further made evident by his consideration of the previously discussed ethics of care. In contrast to the justice principle, which is defined by its focus on equality, equity, and fairness, the principle of benevolence is associated with "Christian ethical teaching" or "agape" and the religiously held notions of "charity," "brotherhood," "sisterhood," and "community." Further, he admits that "the principle of care or responsible love has not been adequately represented in our work."[48] Nonetheless, he still places questions of care under the mantle of cognition. Kohlberg contends that the justice ethic, which embraces the "concepts" of reciprocity and contract, is capable of handling the situational realities (e.g., relationships and personal conflicts) raised by an ethic of benevolence. Yet he also contends that another meaning of moral, which he terms "special" obligations and relationships, is capable of resolving difficulties arising out of particular relationships. Although Kohlberg acknowledges, in effect, two uses of the word "moral" — one embracing the justice ethic and the attributes of impartiality and consensual dialogue and a second defined in terms of caring and altruistic responses accorded special relationships and obligations to family and friends — he points out that the latter is relative and culturally determined. Moreover, Kohlberg maintains that an ethic of care is best viewed as a "personal" use of the word "moral" whereas the justice orientation is moral because of its impartiality and universal application. Kohlberg maintains that these two meanings of "moral" are best viewed as contrasting dimensions of morality, yet he sees the general and universal nature of justice as primary.

As we have noted, however, a glaring deficit in this approach is the stark reality that a principle of justice is unable to account for situations where the issue is not the violation of rights, but questions of love, care, and self-sacrifice (see also Gilligan). As I indicated earlier in this chapter I am continually struck by the fact that when I work with individuals in clinical or pastoral settings, fundamental questions of their self-understanding as moral persons center on attachment, care, and degree of sacrifice rather than on an abstract definition of justice that defines rights and duties (though these dimensions are important for the moral dialogue). The adult child agonizing over sending her elderly parent to a nursing home, the parents struggling over how to handle a troubled adolescent, a married couple trying to negotiate their expectations as loving spouses, a friend trying to understand the breaking of confidentiality by another friend: these are vital questions that go to the core of our experience of the self as moral. It is these very psychic investments in varying relational commitments that express our deepest affections and offer the groundwork for our experience of being moral. It is our very psychic investments in roles of significant relational commitments (e.g., friend, spouse, parent, child, worker) that portray our deepest affections and core sense of self as moral persons.

A related area of concern is Kohlberg's emphasis on reasoning rather than behavior. Kohlberg acknowledges that reasoning is only one factor in determining one's morality, yet he believes it to be the most significant factor. To Kohlberg's credit, in recent years he has shifted more to the necessity of focusing on concrete and practical applications of moral stage development. Thus he and his associates have reported studies that note the success of developing a just community in school situations. Though originally focused simply on group discussions, Kohlberg came to believe that a truly "just" community environment must include participation of faculty, staff, and students in various aspects of decision making as well as the development of a truly "just" (moral) atmosphere. Again, it is to Kohlberg's credit that he has explored the need for a communal school environment that struggles to give meaning to the justice ethic. Nonetheless, even these school environments are controversial. Such environments tend to downplay value content and provide excessive focus on moral discussion. A school community adopting Kohlberg's model can spend so much time processing and conversing over justice issues that the very content of moral principles become secondary. Educational settings are in need of clear and articulated moral norms to which the educational institution subscribes. Moreover, there is need for adults to model and endorse fundamental values (honesty, altruism) without which no community over time could properly function. Certainly, there is need for student input and discussion over moral concerns. Yet such discussion can never be used as a substitute for the endorsement of commonly agreed upon traditional values.[49] Jerome Kagan astutely addresses this issue when he notes the importance of the school's "moral function." Kagan notes

> I believe the schools can play an ameliorative role by providing opportunities for adolescents to persuade themselves of their virtue through acts whose benevolent consequences are not so dependent upon chance, the vicissitudes of peer and adult opinion, or the relative competence of others.[50]

Note Kagan's focus on *action*. He goes on to state the "dimensions of character" that are vital for the school community to uphold. These include "kindness, restraint on aggression, honesty, and a reasonable blend of pride and humility."[51] Kohlberg's just community approach, though admirable, must still consider the essential needs for content and action within the school community.

   Kohlberg's willingness to focus on behavioral linkages to moral reasoning stages in all likelihood should allow for some rapprochement with critics who favor a focus on behaviors. Nevertheless, Kohlberg's adamant stance against any endorsement of an approach to morality that favors traditional virtues and behaviors remains a cause for concern.

In fact, though Kohlberg used the failure of the "bag of virtues" approach as an impetus for his own work, social psychologist Philippe Rushton reexamined the original Hartshorne and May data and found serious flaws in their conclusion that a "bag of virtues" approach is unable to account for moral behavior. In other words, a reconsideration of the data shows that Kohlberg's original dismissal of this classic study is questionable. Hartshorne and May compared student scores on individual test batteries (groups of items together) rather than combined test batteries. Individual test comparisons led to an inflated error variance that is reduced when test batteries are combined. (Variance is the randomness found in any item. The more items included, the more the variance is averaged out across the measure and hence the more accurate the test.) For example, Hartshorne and May compared single tests of altruism separately rather than combining them into a single battery for comparison with other batteries. These single-test comparisons led to naturally low relationships. As Rushton points out, to take tests separately and use them as the basis for analysis is like taking a single question on an academic test and using it as the basis for knowledge. A much more accurate approach is to take several questions and use them as the basis for judging one's ability. This latter approach is not only in all likelihood a more accurate measure of one's knowledge, it is also a more fair assessment of the test taker's knowledge.

These reinterpreted findings led Rushton to conclude that although situations do influence behavior, there exists a consistent moral self and that "the evidence is very solid that there are quite stable and consistent patterns of individual differences across situations."[52] In other words, some people do indeed show a fairly consistent pattern of altruistic living in a wide variety of situations. Of course, no person will behave altruistically across all situations. The pressures of environments, one's own needs, and one's interpretation of a situation all tend to various degrees to influence one's behavior. Based on his findings, Rushton concludes that some people are

> more motivated to engage in altruistic acts. He or she has internalized higher and more universal standards of justice, social responsibility, and modes of moral reasoning, judgment, and knowledge, and/or he or she is more empathic to the feelings and suffering of others and able to see the world from their emotional and motivational perspective. On the basis of such motivations, this person is likely to value, and to engage in, a great variety of altruistic behaviors — from giving to people

more needy than themselves, to comforting others, to rescuing others from aversive situations.[53]

From Rushton's findings we can conclude that there does exist a behavioral tendency for caring that is not limited simply to various situations and places. These reinterpreted findings do not mean that people are consistently caring in every situation. Behaviors are the product of a complex interaction of individual life history, biological endowment, the current situation, the environment, the person's perception of the world, as well as the experience of one's self (habits, personal emotions, etc.). On the other hand, we need not accept Kohlberg's interpretation of altruistic acts as dependent upon the situation.

Having set forth the viable nature of a consistent moral orientation oriented to care, we must provide a psychological basis for this caring response and show how such a basis is in harmony with the Christian moral vision. This is our task in the chapters ahead.

Conclusion

In this chapter we have examined the current state of a "psychology of morality." We have taken a critical look at the dominant perspective in this field: Lawrence Kohlberg's theory of moral development. Kohlberg has proven an invaluable resource for educators, psychologists, and religious professionals. First, he has linked empirical research and philosophical speculation in a fashion that will be the benchmark for future ventures. Second, Kohlberg's work has shown us the complexity of morality. Constructing a moral identity is by its very nature a developmental process. Finally, Kohlberg's work has provided a compelling rationale for morality. More than anything, he has presented us with the vital role that rational reflection exercises in the moral quest.

Nonetheless, as we have seen, Kohlberg's thinking is limited. Given his view of morality, those inclined toward a Christian vision of morality need to exercise serious caution. The richness of a moral sense that every person desires and hungers for is reduced in Kohlberg's schema to a confining rationality that is unable to appreciate the rich complexity of the moral life. Summing up this view, one critic has written that "one suspects that if this theory is to continue to have a major influence on research on moral development, future theory building needs to integrate the cognitive with the behavioral and affective components of morality and needs to be built on a firm empirical base."[54]

The task is not as grand as developing a new moral theory. Yet the focus of the discussion remains significant. In the chapters ahead I will offer an integrated view of how developmental theorizing and research provide for moral experience that resonates with the Christian moral vision.

➤ *Chapter 3* ≺

Empathy: Morality's Heart

One can hope that a disciplined and value-oriented social science will have sufficient time not only to study and understand the nature and determinants of empathy but also to develop the ability to increase the number of human beings who are functionally empathic. If this is done, there will be a future for humanity. The survival of the human species now appears to depend upon a universal increase in functional empathy. Trained human intelligence must now dedicate itself to the attainment of this goal.

—Kenneth B. Clark

Searching for a Moral Path

The issue of morality has received increasing interest in the public arena. Social philosopher Michael Novak has remarked that "the nation's return to this discussion [of morality] is one of the decisive events of the last twenty years."[1] A recent Gallup poll suggests that the overwhelming majority of American parents support the discussion of morality within the American school system. Higher education has also attempted to respond to this renewed interest. Currently, in any given year, America's institutions of higher learning offer eleven thousand courses in areas of applied ethics over a wide variety of disciplines.[2]

The renewed interest in morality arises in part from recent disclosures of questionable moral practices. National attention has focused on investigations of corruption at both the federal and local levels, questionable business practices (e.g., of Wall Street brokerage firms), and sports scandals at major universities throughout the country.

Furthermore, according to a national Roper survey, one of four Americans admits cheating on his or her income tax returns. Resulting lost revenue to the federal government is estimated at well over 135 billion dollars. In addition, in the private sector it is estimated that employers lose 160 billion dollars annually because of individuals who misuse work time.[3]

In light of the above, the question of honesty, the nature of helpfulness, and a basic orientation that limits egoistic concerns and the desire for personal aggrandizement are issues of significance for American society. Morality as justice is insufficient. Traditional values and an orientation to care are vital ingredients for society's moral health. As philosopher Christina Hoff Sommers notes, "too little attention is paid to the personal aspects of morality — courage, compassion, generosity, honor and self-respect, or, on the negative side, hypocrisy, self-deception, jealousy and narcissism." [4] In short, the very basic questions posed by the Hartshorne and May studies a half century ago are vital questions for us still. An essential orientation to care and to values reflecting this care are needed for society's everyday functioning.

Studies indicate that when people offer their own understanding of what constitutes a moral dilemma, they express it in terms that point to an ethics of care and everyday traditional values, rather than to the rule-oriented and life-death situations portrayed by Kohlberg's cognitive-developmental approach.[5] For example, when students are asked to write about moral dilemmas they are decidedly relational in character. Commenting upon one example of this research, two authors concluded that

> most of the stories in this study involved characters who were the same age and sex as the students who wrote the stories, whereas Kohlberg's stories are chiefly male and adult-oriented. Kohlberg's vignettes are hypothetical and abstract, whereas the students in our sample wrote stories involving practical everyday experiences. Furthermore, Kohlberg's stories emphasize conflicts between individuals and societal values, whereas the stories in our sample stressed relationship issues.[6]

The conclusion from these studies is clear. When thinking about morality, the tendency is to think in terms of relationships. Questions of care and the quality of the relationship are what is crucial, and these questions demand an understanding of empathy.

No doubt Kohlberg's cognitive-developmental theory remains the dominant perspective from which to view a psychology of morality. Yet, recent advances in developmental theory have raised alternative approaches. Kohlberg has argued for an ontogenetic understanding of the justice principle as the basis for morality. Other researchers have maintained that it is possible to look for a source of morality that is emotion-based. The most promising source for this view of morality is the construct of empathy. It is to this view of morality that we now turn.

I will examine shortly a more detailed explanation of empathy. For now, however, I simply wish to note that empathy's import arises from an essential bondedness. Empathy underscores an experience of interrelationship. In essence, it serves as an essential ingredient for fostering caring interpersonal functioning, the very issues at the heart of Gilligan's argument for an ethics of care. There are few more stark expressions of this essential bondedness than Shylock's pleading in William Shakespeare's *The Merchant of Venice.*

> he hath disgrac'd me, and hind'red me half a million, laugh'd at my losses, mock'd at my gains, scorned my nation, thwarted my bargains, cooled my friends, heated mine enemies, — and what's his reason? I am a Jew. Hath not a Jew eyes? hath not a Jew hands, organs, dimensions, senses, affections, passions? fed with the same food, hurt with the same weapons, subject to the same diseases, healed by the same means, warmed and cooled by the same winter and summer as a Christian is? — if you prick us do we not bleed? if you tickle us do we not laugh? if you poison us do we not die? and if you wrong us shall we not revenge? — if we are like you in the rest, we will resemble you in that.[7]

This powerful statement affirming a Jew's humanity derives its force from the empathic tone it elicits. A reader cannot help but feel bonded to Shylock and his situation, moved by his struggle and plight. Empathy draws one into an *existential solidarity* with Shylock. Indeed, empathy is the foundational soil that roots one's solidarity with another's life and struggle. The reader's empathy forges a bond between the self and Shylock; a relationship emerges that elicits care and concern.

Empathy becomes particularly important when considering the current state of American culture. Sociologist Gerald Grant, commenting on the character of the American school, notes that the emphasis placed heretofore on value neutrality has led to a crisis in

American education. "The crisis of authority in the American school is that in many places we no longer have any agreement on what that provisional morality ought to be."[8] By provisional morality Grant means a socialization to "some set of standards, beliefs, and values about what it means to be a human being"[9] that can be reevaluated by the child when he or she reaches adulthood. The point to be made, though, is that the educational system is unable to reach consensus on what such a morality might be. As a consequence, schools have for too long avoided moral content and fostered a value neutrality. As a solution, Grant advocates a recommitment to a provisional morality that distinctly champions positive behaviors associated with a morality based on care and traditional values. He argues that a provisional morality must "express some of the conscious beliefs of a democratic pluralist society."[10] Characteristics of such a morality include

> the minimal order required for dialogue, the willingness to listen to one another, respect for truth, the rejection of racism (or openness to participation in the dialogue), as well as those transcendent values that shore up the whole society — a sense of altruism and service to others and respect for personal effort and hard work. Without such an agreement, one does not have a public, but a kind of radical, relativism; not pluralism but mere coexistence.[11]

In a similar vein, psychologist Jerome Kagan, as noted in the previous chapter, has maintained that the American school exercises a critical function for the American community. He argues that a responsibility of the school is to develop a "dimension of character" among students. He describes the characteristics critical for such character dimension:

> Thus I borrow from both the moral absolutists as well as the utilitarians in suggesting the dimensions of character to be celebrated at least until the balance is restored. Kindness, restraint on aggression, honesty, and a reasonable blend of pride and humility stand at the top of my list for several reasons. First, the community currently needs more citizens to practice these standards, and many youth are dissatisfied with the callous acts of privacy, cheating, lying, and, on rare occasions, destruction of a peer's notes they are forced to in order to survive in a system that can award special merit to only a few. But my observations of children persuade me that kindness and control of aggression

have a natural priority in development. Three-year-olds spontaneously offer toys to peers in distress and are reluctant to strike
another, unless the latter intrudes or threatens.[12]

In a similar vein, philosopher Alasdair MacIntyre has characterized the current state of moral thinking as one of moral disarray. He
notes the contemporary state of morality is one "of grave disorder."
According to MacIntyre, contemporary culture lacks a consensual
understanding of morality and thereby provides no uniform rationale for deciding moral disputes. "For what analysis of A's and B's
position reveals once again is that we have all too many disparate and
rival moral concepts."[13] In essence, the idea of a moral community
has been lost and opposing views of justice vie for dominance, each
moral ideology with its adherents.

This fragmenting of community, which MacIntyre discusses in
terms of moral philosophy, is taken up by sociologist Robert Bellah
and reframed in light of sociological insight. Commenting upon the
ethical quandary that exists today, Bellah notes:

> Now if selves are defined by their preferences, but those pref-
> erences are arbitrary, then each self constitutes its own moral
> universe, and there is finally no way to reconcile conflicting
> claims about what is good in itself.... In the absence of any ob-
> jectifiable criteria of right and wrong, good or evil, the self and
> its feelings become our only moral guide. What kind of world is
> inhabited by this self, perpetually in progress, yet without any
> fixed moral end?[14]

Historically, says Bellah, the dominant ethos in American culture
has been the focus on "individualism." In short, individualism in both
its utilitarian form (the personal maximization of goods) and its expressive form (the primacy of self-actualized feelings) has sundered
the individual from his or her historically felt rootings in community. Consequently, Americans remain deeply ambivalent about their
individualism.

> The inner tensions of American individualism add up to a clas-
> sic case of ambivalence. We strongly assert the value of our
> self-reliance and autonomy. We deeply feel the emptiness of a
> life without sustaining social commitments. Yet we are hesitant
> to articulate our sense that we need one another as much as

we need to stand alone, for fear that if we did we would lose
independence altogether.[15]

The philosophical quandary and social strains flowing from disparate moral positions and the dominance of individualism in American culture will not be resolved here. Yet to pose the presence of a
morality based on care and bondedness, whose foundation is empathy, and that in turn fosters altruistic behaviors, provides a consensual
basis for moral dialogue as well as a bridge for discussion among diverse beliefs and autonomous human behaviors. That is, although
individuals reason to conflictual moral views and subsequently engage in contradictory if not opposing behaviors, all individuals are
endowed with an empathic sense and a generally agreed upon consensus that a minimal level of prosocial conduct is necessary for personal
and societal functioning.

Bellah's discussion of how Americans understand and express
their sensitivity and care offers insight into how empathy might provide increased moral understanding. American life is best characterized as "a society in which the individual can only rarely and
with difficulty understand himself and his activities as interrelated in
morally meaningful ways with those of other, different Americans."[16]
As such, individualism is "the dominant ideology of American life."[17]
A consequence of individualism's dominating presence is the relega-
tion at times of caring behavior to some form of enlightened self-
interest. The ethos of individualism encourages one to respond to
the other's needs if and only if, all things considered, such actions
benefit oneself.

Because empathy includes both cognitive and affective components, prosocial behavior engendered by empathic arousal provides
an optimum forum for encouraging both self-awareness and positive
social interactions. All in all, given proper social reinforcement and
environmental supports, empathic expressions would provide a useful
antidote to the impoverished understandings of prosocial inclinations
that are commonly expressed in American life.

The Meaning of Empathy

The idea that empathy is essential for morality has a rich heritage in
Western thought. "For at least 300 years philosophers in the Anglo-
American (or utilitarian) tradition of ethics have assumed that man
has an innate social sensitivity which plays an important role in moral
development."[18] Historically, philosophers such as David Hume and

Adam Smith as well as social scientists such as George Herbert Mead have accorded a significant role to empathy in their own theories.

The origin of the word "empathy" can be traced from the German word *Einfühlung*, most aptly translated as "feeling into." The word *Einfühlung* was introduced into psychological literature by Theodor Lipps in his discussion of aesthetic perception. Originally, Lipps viewed the person as projecting himself or herself into an object; as a consequence, the perceiver developed a far deeper appreciative understanding of the object at hand. Later, Lipps widened his definition to include people as the objects of focus. The notion of empathic understanding arose from the observer's reaction to the observed person's behavior. In effect, the perceiver provided cues that served as signals for his or her newly found understanding of the other person.[19]

In 1910 the experimental psychologist Edward Titchener translated the word *Einfühlung* as "empathy."

His influence was great. His erudition was massive. His competence in modern languages, as well as Greek and Latin, was considerable. And his interest in etymology led him to translate *Einfühlung* as "empathy" via the Greek *empatheia*, which means literally "in" (*en*) "suffering or passion" (*pathos*). *Einfühlung* means "to feel one's way into," and the etymological similarity between empathy and sympathy did not escape Titchener.[20]

Though there appears great similarity between sympathy and empathy, they are not the same.

When we examine another term in the German language, *Mitfühlung* (sympathy) in relation to *Einfühlung*, we can see the implications of the [empathy] concept clearly. *Mit* in this context must be translated as 'along with' rather than 'together with.' A sympathetic person feels *along with* another person but not necessarily *into* a person. ... Empathic behavior implies a convergence. ... Sympathetic behavior implies a parallelism in the behavior of two individuals.[21]

At the beginning of this century the term "empathy" was first used to describe an aesthetic experience that arose while viewing a piece of art. Moreover, through the years "empathy" has come to have significance in the fields of personality theory, developmental psychology, and counseling. By mid-century use of "empathy" in counseling gained ascendance, particularly as a result of the influence of Carl

Rogers. Rogers has suggested that empathy was best viewed as a necessary ingredient for successful therapeutic interaction between therapist and client. He defined empathy as: "to perceive the internal frame of reference of another with accuracy, and with the emotional components and meanings that pertain thereto, as if one were the other person, but without ever losing the 'as if' condition."[22]

Recently, studies of therapeutic interactions between clients and therapists have moved beyond Rogers's phenomenological definition of empathy and have considered empathy more as a "process" of responding to the client's experience rather than as the vicariously aroused state of the therapist. Moreover, this change in research strategies reveals the priority given to communicating to the client and the awareness of one's understanding of what is happening within the therapeutic relationship.[23]

One inevitable aspect of empathy research is the plethora of definitions available. Harold Hackney notes the existence of twenty-one definitions.[24] Psychologists Arnold Goldstein and Gerald Michaels list sixteen various definitions of the term.[25] Though the variation is great, empathy usually has one or more of the following components: (a) an emotional component; (b) a cognitive component; (c) and/or a communication of one's feeling state to the other.

My own preference is to resist adopting a definitional understanding of therapeutic empathy and to favor for the most part a definition of empathy as defined in developmental theory, it is an understanding in line with an ethics of care. Consequently, we will discuss in detail the most sophisticated treatment of this term by examining the work of psychologist Martin Hoffman.

Martin Hoffman's Theory of Empathic Development

Martin Hoffman has proposed the most integrated and conceptually coherent theory of empathic development.[26] Empathy's significance for moral understanding is best viewed by considering its role in the development of altruism. Hoffman has looked at empathy as the foundation for an altruistic view of human nature.[27] He notes that anthropological evidence indicates that prehistoric individuals encountered an adverse and hostile environment; evolution provides two motives that have enabled the human species to survive. On the one hand, there exists the egoistic motive of self-protection or the enhancement of one's own condition. On the other hand, there exists an independent altruistic motive that promotes the other's welfare "without conscious regard for one's own self-interest."[28] Hoffman envisions empathy as the source of this care for others. Accordingly, both an egoistic motive and an altruistic motive are necessary, as both motive systems allow for an optimal level of human adaptability and, therefore, of human survival.

The validity of an independent altruistic motive, says Hoffman, comes from research that documents individuals' spontaneously helping others, particularly when they are the only persons available to aid the distressed person. But if the basis of altruistic responding resides in egoism, then one would expect individuals in need of social approval to help more than others who feel satisfied with their level of social approval. In fact, the research supports the opposite conclusion; that is, individuals who are satisfied with their own social approval are most likely to engage in altruistic acts. A likely reason for this phenomenon is that individuals who are dissatisfied with their social standing are likely to be "needy" emotionally. Therefore, they adopt ego defensive strategies and utilize their psychic energies to deal with feelings of inadequacy. Consequently, they are less likely to be attentive to the needs of others, having focused their psychic energies on their own troubled emotional states.

Finally, there exists biological evidence to support the presence of an altruistic motive. Hoffman cites studies by MacLean that focus on the limbic system's effect on expressive and feeling states.[29] Hoffman notes that part of the limbic system (that portion of the brain associated with emotion and sex and hunger drives) appears to be related to prosociality and the development of social bondedness. MacLean reports that one area of the limbic system is associated with emotions that foster self-preservation. In addition, however, MacLean maintains another area of the limbic system is predisposed to sociability. He notes that "in the complex organization of the old and new structures under consideration, we presumably have a neural ladder, a visionary ladder, for ascending from the most primitive sexual feelings to the highest level of altruistic sentiments."[30] In addition, the study of the brain appears to sustain the biological possibility for altruism. MacLean has shown that a neural connection exists among the primitive limbic cortex, the hypothalamus (which integrates somatic experiences and feeling states), and the prefrontal cortex (which fosters insight and an awareness of others' needs). Says Hoffman:

> In other words, the brain structures required for affective involvement with objects in the external world, including people, were apparently present early in man's evolution. The more

recent addition of newer brain structures along with the acquisition of connective neural circuits have made it possible for
such affect to be experienced in conjunction with a cognitive,
increasingly sophisticated social awareness or insight into others — and all of this appears to be independent of the neural
base for egoistic, self-preserving behavior. In brief, the neural
basis for a primitive empathy was apparently present early in
man's evolution.[31]

In sum, the presence of a sophisticated empathic response requires
the presence of advanced neurocortical development and adequate
limbic system functioning. Thus there is within the human species a
biological foundation for empathic experience.

Moreover, growth in empathy appears to be related to central
nervous system development.[32] Psychiatrist Leslie Brothers has discussed the complex interplay of biological factors associated with
empathy, particularly as it pertains to the "visual pathway of information." Drawing upon a wide range of clinical data, Brothers suggests
relationships among neural processes, patterns of social communication, and the nature of the visual pathway. She states:

Because of this confluence of data from a variety of disciplines, empathy (a subjective experience between people),
social-emotional communication (in animals) and social signal
processing (by neurons) can be understood as aspects of a single
phenomenon. The phenomenon in man appears to be a product of both species evolution and individual history. Empathy,
then, is a biological concept par excellence whose full analysis depends on understanding historically interdependent social,
somatic, and intrapsychic events.[33]

All in all, the varying pieces of evidence lend support to an altruistic motive in human social exchanges. Given that this is the case,
Hoffman inquires as to what is the mediator or mechanism that fosters altruistic behavior and concludes that empathy is the most likely
mediator for an altruistic response.

The Components and Modes of Empathy

According to Hoffman, empathy is best defined as "an affective response more appropriate to someone else's situation than to one's
own."[34] With this definition one's own response does not necessarily duplicate the other's, yet is similar to it. This "appropriateness"

is derived from the cognitive component of empathy, which allows for an accurate interpretation of another's state. Thus, for example, if one perceived another's injury as arising from laziness or from callous behavior, one would not be inclined to empathize with the person's plight. But if the injury arose from grave injustice or an unforeseen tragic accident, then one's natural tendencies toward empathy would be triggered. The central experience of empathy is the emotional arousal experienced by the empathizer. Furthermore, in addition to emotional arousal, empathy appears closely linked to a naturally induced state to respond altruistically to another's distress.

Hoffman notes that "it should not be surprising that empathy appears to be a universal, largely involuntary response — if one attends to the relevant cues one responds empathically — that may have had survival value in human evolution."[35]

Moreover, empathy's power is often irresistible when confronted with highly salient situations ("relevant cues") where one perceives the needs of others. This empathic experience is portrayed vividly in John Cheever's poignant story, *Christmas Is a Sad Season for the Poor*. Cheever describes the wrenching experience of impoverished parents who must struggle to provide presents for their children and the pained perplexity of children who must make sense of their crushed expectations. Speaking of the children in the ghettos, he writes:

They got the worst of it. Beginning in the fall, there was all this excitement about Christmas and how it was a day for them. After Thanksgiving, they couldn't miss it. It was fixed so they couldn't miss it. The wreaths and decorations everywhere, and bells ringing, and trees in the park, and Santa Clauses on every corner, and pictures in the magazines and newspapers and on every wall and window in the city told them that if they were good, they would get what they wanted. Even if they couldn't read, they couldn't miss it. They couldn't miss it even if they were blind. It got into the air the poor kids inhaled. Every time they took a walk, they'd see all the expensive toys in the store windows, and they'd write letters to Santa Claus, and their mothers and fathers would promise to mail them, and after the kids had gone to sleep, they'd burn the letters in the stove. And when it came Christmas morning, how could you explain it, how could you tell them that Santa Claus only visited the rich, that he didn't know about the good? How could you face them when all you had to give them was a balloon or a lollipop?[36]

As you read this excerpt what did you as a reader experience? Did your "heart" not go out to the anguish of parents whose tormented grief is so wrenching? If you were the parent of such a child, how would you feel? Did you not experience the feeling of powerlessness Cheever's parents felt or perhaps even outrage at why individuals must suffer so painfully (what Hoffman terms "empathic anger")? Is there not an irresistible urge to eradicate the pained disappointment on the faces of these children as they grope with their thwarted yet so human need to receive? Did not the season of Christmas itself trigger feelings ("relevant cues")? Indeed, does not the season of Christmas (environmental cue) engender empathic responses that border on emotional contagion? To illustrate, follow again Cheever as he ends this story with the entreaty of a poor parent who, upon receiving many gifts during the season, is bitten with the need to look out for the needs of others who are even more destitute. At the right moment (in this case, Christmas day) empathy's lure is overwhelming:

"Now, you kids have had enough already," she said. "You kids have got your share. Just look at the things you got there. Why, you ain't even played with the half of them. Mary Anne, you ain't even looked at that doll the Fire Department give you. Now, a nice thing to do would be to take all this stuff that's left over to those poor people on Hudson Street — them Deckkers. They ain't got nothing." A beatific light came into her face when she realized that she could give, that she could bring them cheer, that she could put a healing finger on a case needier than hers, and — like Mrs. DePaul and Mrs. Weston, like Charlie himself and like Mrs. Deckker, when Mrs. Deckker was to think, subsequently, of the poor Shannons — first love, then charity, and then a sense of power drove her. "Now, you kids help me get all this stuff together. Hurry, hurry, hurry," she said, for it was dark then, and she knew that we are bound, one to another, in licentious benevolence for only a single day, and that day was nearly over. She was tired, but she couldn't rest, she couldn't rest.[37]

As the above passage powerfully portrays, all in all, given the right time and context, one becomes particularly responsive to the distress and pain of others and is moved to respond in caring ways to the other's plight.

Hoffman maintains that through the course of human development, six modes of empathic arousal emerge. These modes are discussed below.

Reactive Newborn Cry. Developmental studies demonstrate that even three-day-old infants utter reactive cries upon hearing the cries of other infants. Although it is impossible to state whether such reactions are learned or innate, it has been shown that infants respond to the distressed cry of other infants. "This reactive cry must therefore be considered as a possible early precursor of empathy, though not a full empathic response because it lacks any awareness of what is happening."[38] In other words, developmentally, the newborn lacks the ability to comprehend the actual situation of the others, yet even this tendency demonstrates an orientation, if only rudimentary, to the needs of others.

Classical Conditioning. Soon after the experience of the reactive cry, the infant can view the distress of another at the same time that he or she is experiencing distress. Conditioning (it is helpful to view "conditioned" as an experience of learning) results from the fact that "distress cues from others become conditioned stimuli that evoke feelings of distress in the self."[39] Hoffman offers as an example the tenseness of a mother who, upon holding her child, conditions an anxious state in the child. At a later time, the mother's facial or verbal cues that accompany her distress (conditioned stimuli) trigger distress in the child even in the absence of physical contact.

Direct Association. A more general type of conditioning exists through an association. This third mode of empathic arousal is contingent upon the past experience of the one who empathizes. In other words, the distress cues of another evoke in the child his or her past experiences of distress, which in turn induce an empathic response.

> The feelings of distress that accompanied those past experiences are then evoked by distress cues from the victim that call up any of them. It is thus a far more general mechanism than conditioning, one that may provide the basis for a variety of distress experiences with which children and adults as well may empathize.[40]

Evidence for this experience of direct association is suggested by individuals' donations to charity. Data indicate that the poor give in a disproportionately generous way to charitable causes:

> People with incomes under $10,000 give 2.8 percent of what they have, and those at $10,000 to $30,000 give 2.5 percent. At the other end of the scale, people with incomes of $50,000 to $75,000 give 1.5 percent; $75,000 to $100,000 give 1.7 per-

cent; and $100,000 or more, 2.1 percent. One-half of what is contributed comes from families with incomes under $30,000.[41]

Though there might be numerous interpretations of these figures, a most plausible one is, simply, that those who struggle financially, given their own suffering, are more apt to be aroused empathically and contribute generously. Aware of their own suffering, when confronted by the plight of others they respond in a most caring manner. The story of the Widow's Mite (Luke 21:1–4) makes, therefore, good psychological sense. Like her counterparts today, she responds altruistically and is most generous.

Mimicry. In this mode of empathic arousal a person imitates the facial features and posture of another person. This imitation in turn leads to "inner kinesthetic cues" that aid the observer in understanding the other and allow for the feeling of similar emotions. Heretofore, this mode of empathy has been passed over because of its instinctual overtones; Hoffman, however, views it as a plausible empathic experience.

Symbolic Association. A more advanced mode of empathic arousal is associated with symbolization. In this mode a person becomes aware of another's distress through symbols (e.g., reading a letter). Thus, language mediates between the empathizing observer and the distress of the victim. An example of this mode of empathic expression comes from documenting behaviors following tragic accidents. For example, following the fatal bombing of a Pan American jet in December 1988, families of the victims were deluged with condolences and expressions of support from those who read about the tragedy. One family in Massachusetts received letters from strangers as far away as California and London expressing their sympathy.[42] The outpouring of care most likely is derived from symbolic association (reading about the tragedy), which in turn engenders empathic arousal and the desire to offer solace to the distressed relatives of the victims.

Role-taking. Empathic experiences associated with the previous five modes require only minimum cognitive effort. Role-taking (taking the perspective of another), on the other hand, the most developmentally advanced of the empathic modes, requires an individual to imagine how he or she would feel in the other's situation. This imaging of the other's situation leads one to "experience some of what the other person is feeling."[43]

Hoffman does not view these six modes as equally utilized in everyday life situations; rather, reactive crying is shed with devel-

opment, whereas role-taking is infrequently utilized. The four inter-
mediate modes are used intermittently throughout the life span and
require a variety of situational cues for their activation. Hoffman
maintains that empathy has three basic components: cognitive, affective, and motivational. This threefold delineation is crucial inasmuch
as most definitions of empathy underscore cognitive and affective dimensions yet fail to focus on subsequent behaviors that reduce the
plight of the distressed person.

A large amount of empirical evidence has been gathered to support
Hoffman's view that empathy is a basis for altruistic action. Based
on research that is now a decade old, Ervin Staub, in a comprehensive review of positive social behavior, has stated that although "it is
difficult to demonstrate convincingly the mediating influence of empathy on helping,"[44] a cumulative review of the research does "suggest
that empathy is a likely determinant of helping."[45] Social psychologist
Philippe Rushton has maintained that empathy is a vital ingredient
in the formation of an "altruistic personality."[46] Major studies and
reviews of prosocial behavior over the past decade consistently point
to the critical role that empathy exercises in the formation of caring
behavior.[47]

At the same time, although researchers generally conclude that empathy is a vital component for prosocial responding, the relationship
between empathy and prosocial behavior is complex. Inconsistencies
are found in studies measuring the role of empathy and prosocial
responding in children; when the analysis turns to adults, a more uniform picture of the consistency of empathy and caring surfaces. Differences among children result from the fact that they are less likely to
interpret accurately situations calling for empathic responses. Further,
children often are incapable of knowing just what is the appropriate
helping response, or lack the awareness required for implementing a
caring response.

Although numerous researchers have linked empathic development and prosocial responding, no theorist has maintained that empathy alone is sufficient to bring about caring behavior. In this regard,
Eisenberg has noted that the adolescent can justify his or her personal behavior by a diverse array of reasons (rationalizations) ranging
from hedonistic desires to internalized moral principles and that "in
real life, situations that call for prosocial actions vary across many
dimensions."[48] Further, Hoffman has concluded that "although one's
empathic proclivities may make one more receptive to certain moral
values, empathy alone cannot explain how people formulate complex
moral ideologies and apply them in situations."[49]

Moreover, a wide variety of factors must be taken into consideration when one attempts to analyze why people respond in caring ways. These include developmental level (the capacity for certain responses such as "empathy"), mood, the situation, social influences, one's personal philosophy (which would include values, ideology, and attitudes), and environmental supports.

As the above list would suggest, the question for researchers is not whether empathic arousal is linked to altruistic acts, but under what conditions is empathy most likely to induce caring responses.

The Development of Empathy

Hoffman maintains that the cognitive transformation of empathy transpires developmentally. Hoffman's "model also posits an important role for cognitive processes in the experience of affective empathy. The particular cognitive process that Hoffman's model is concerned with is that of the child's maturing ability to differentiate self from others."[50] Hoffman's theory sets forth four developmental levels of empathic distress.

Global Empathy. Essentially, before the year one, the child lacks the capacity to differentiate the self from others. Thus the child, upon viewing the distress of the other, is unable to construe the distressed person's plight as separate from his or her own and, therefore, he or she acts accordingly. This empathic response is termed global because the child fails to differentiate between the discomfort of others and his or her own distress; thus, distress is experienced as a diffuse and generalized state encompassing both the distressed person as well as the infant.

"Egocentric Empathy." Having obtained "person permanence,"[51] the child is capable of differentiating the self from others thereby understanding that the distress of the other is not his or her own. At this stage a child is most likely to respond to the other's distress by sharing an object or engaging in behavior that relieves the child's own distress. Hoffman cites as an example the thirteen-month-old child who, upon seeing the distress of the adult, offers the adult his favorite toy. I witnessed an example of this phenomenon. While attending a class reunion of my former students, I noticed that the fifteen-month-old child of one student tried to give her own doll to another child who was crying. Similarly, on a personal note, my mother recalls the story of how my older sister, who was eighteen months old at the time, placed all her own toys in the crib just before I was brought home from the hospital. All of these instances point to a spontaneous act of care, even though the young child is unable to

offer the appropriate response. Insofar as egocentrism is present, the child does confuse actions that offer relief to the other with actions that lessen the child's own distress. Nonetheless, both the affective tone of the child's utterances and his or her facial cues as well as the behavior itself clearly point to a developmentally appropriate caring response (that is, the child utilizes whatever psychological resources are available and responds appropriately).

Empathy for Another's Feeling. Although at first rudimentary, the inception of role-taking allows the two- or three-year-old child to begin to appreciate the other's feelings and interpretations of events as separate from his or her own. At the same time, the child's language development allows for an increased consciousness and sensitivity to the feelings of others. Finally, with development, the child becomes increasingly sophisticated at differentiating the feeling of others and empathizing simultaneously with diverse feelings.

Although not directly addressing the question of empathy, developmental research demonstrates that very young children show a remarkable level of caring behavior, thereby lending support to Hoffman's contention that there is an altruistic dimension to human nature. These findings run contrary to earlier theoretical pronouncements (e.g., Freud) that maintained that human nature was riddled with unconscious conflicts and selfishness. In fact, given the possibility of caring behavior, even among very young children (as young as two years old), it can be concluded that empathy theorists would argue that very young children are capable of rudimentary moral responses. True to the nature of developmental thinking, empathy theorists would ultimately maintain that although the young child is incapable of sophisticated moral explanations of his or her action, the fact that he or she responds at whatever capacity he or she is capable of points to a general moral orientation. Moreover, with time, the child's empathic expression takes on greater sophistication.

> Empathizing with a victim's distress, children may also eventually become capable of empathizing with the victim's anxiety about the loss of self-esteem, hence with the desire *not* to be helped. Finally, children can be empathically aroused by information about someone's distress even in that person's absence. This leads to the fourth, most advanced level.[52]

Empathy for Another's General Plight. By the later childhood years, the young person or early adolescent is capable of understanding that other people possess independent life histories, that immediate feelings are oftentimes transitory, and that the other person has feelings beyond a particular situation. Thus, at this level, a child can imagine the situation of the other beyond the situation at hand (e.g., the child realizes that an economically deprived peer might be joyful over receiving a birthday gift, yet realize the child remains disadvantaged and continues to endure an impoverished existence). This final level elicits a more sophisticated response from the observer that balances immediate reactions to the other's plight with a fuller understanding of the other's existential situation. Hoffman concludes:

> To summarize, empathy is the coalescence of vicariously aroused affect and a mental representation of the other, at whatever level the observer is capable. Individuals who progress through the four stages become capable of a high level of empathic distress.[53]

Although not considered a level, Hoffman maintains that a more advanced understanding of "Empathy for Another's Plight" allows the child or adolescent to empathize with entire classes or people (e.g., the poor, the oppressed, a racial or ethnic group). This wider domain for empathizing results from abstractive and reasoning abilities coming with the attainment of advanced thinking (formal thought), characterized by deepening reflectivity, future possibility, and abstraction.

Empathy and Compassion

Empathic distress (one's internal reaction to another's plight) has so far been viewed as having both a cognitive and an affective component. These components are "derived from the observer's cognitive sense of the other."[54] Equally important, this enhanced cognitive capacity, in addition to fostering empathic distress, engenders in the observer (the one who is empathizing with the victim) a feeling of sympathetic distress (or what is generally termed compassion). The end result of the observer's awareness of the other and sympathetic distress is an inclination to respond in a caring (prosocial) manner. In other words, as one experiences empathic distress regarding another's plight, there develops concern and the corresponding desire to aid the other.

> That is, they may continue to respond in a purely empathic manner — to feel uncomfortable and highly distressed themselves — but they also experience a feeling of compassion for the victim, along with a conscious desire to help because they feel sorry for the victim and not just to relieve their own empathic distress.[55]

The experience of compassion (sympathetic distress) pinpoints the hallmark of empathy's value: a deeply felt distress arising from concern for the other and engendering aid and support. The power of compassion is seen through a discussion of its etymological roots. Donald McNeill, Douglas Morrison, and Henri Nouwen address this issue directly:

> The word *compassion* is derived from the Latin words *pati* and *cum*, which together mean "to suffer with." Compassion asks us to go where it hurts, to enter into places of pain, to share in brokenness, fear, confusion, and anguish. Compassion challenges us to cry out with those in misery, to mourn with those who are lonely, to weep with those in tears. Compassion requires us to be weak with the weak, vulnerable with the vulnerable, and powerless with the powerless. Compassion means full immersion in the condition of being human.[56]

The type of compassion described here is not "guaranteed" by empathic experience. Even so, *without* the experience of empathy, the very experience of compassion would be impossible. In other words, one's capacity for empathy is the psychological foundation for engendering the compassionate stance. These writers underscore that the suffering that accompanies compassion makes it an experience we resist, an experience alien to us because of the pain involved. "Compassion is not among our most natural responses. We are pain-avoiders and we consider anyone who feels attracted to suffering abnormal, or at least very unusual."[57] Unfortunately, these writers are mistaken about the human spirit. No doubt compassion is an experience that is not consistently shown and requires effort as well as attention to numerous other factors for its full expression. Yet there does exist, as we see with Hoffman's theory, a natural capacity inherent within the human species to suffer with another and to render aid. The key question for developmental researchers and pastoral and ministry professionals is to address the conditions and environmental supports that nurture this empathic sense and sustain its expression throughout life.

Moreover, compassion touches one's core experience of being moral. In some instances it defies any type of rational expression. "It is sometimes the very irrationality of compassion, the residual capacity to respond with tenderness and love when all one's reasons counsel otherwise, that confers upon a compassionate act its sweetness, beauty, and nobility."[58] Such acts originate in the empathic stirrings of the heart and strike at the core of who we are. "It is the compassionate heart that can still somehow make itself felt that makes men's deeds sometimes noble and beautiful, and nothing else at all."[59] It is this empathic urge and its accompanying distress that pierces our consciousness, allowing an ever deepening understanding of our moral sensibilities. A critical catalyst within this entire process is the capacity for guilt.

Empathy and Guilt

In addition to the cognitive and affective components of empathic distress and the concomitant sympathetic distress, Hoffman asserts that guilt exercises a special role in influencing the child's prosocial nature. In all likelihood, a cognitive component is integral to the formation of a guilt response; growth in cognitive abilities enables the child to acquire more sophisticated guilt responses. Thus, cognitive maturation allows the child to view how his or her actions might be the source of another's injury. Thus, even younger children can feel guilty over the observed physical hurt they cause one another. A more developmentally advanced form of cognition is necessary, however, to attribute blame to one's own actions or to feel guilt over the anticipation of hurting the other. Furthermore, "another important cognitive dimension of guilt is the awareness that one has choice and control over one's behavior."[60] Although the evidence on choice is minimal, a plausible explanation, says Hoffman, is the child's realization of his or her omnipotence. In turn, this omnipotence gives way to a sense of helplessness and eventually to an understanding that he or she has the ability to control only to various degrees (depending on the situation) most of his or her actions.

> It seems plausible tentatively to assume that there is an early developmental progression from a sense of omnipotence, to a sense of helplessness, and finally to an awareness of having some but not total control over one's actions.[61]

Another cognitive dimension of guilt arises when the child comes to understand the moral norms of society, specifically the norm against harming another. The child, socialized to this norm, will experience guilt when he or she engages in or contemplates actions that deviate from the norm.

A far more developmentally advanced form of guilt is "existential guilt." This guilt response is classically expressed by the late adolescent (e.g., college freshman) who enters college and is exposed to information and philosophical ideas at variance with his or her middle-class or upper-class background. As a consequence, the student experiences a sense of guilt; that is, the late adolescent comes to believe that his or her privileged position makes one accountable for the distress and plight of others. Having been made aware of others' impoverishment and distress, the late adolescent is capable of empathizing with the disadvantaged while simultaneously feeling guilty over his or her privileged state. In sum, the attribution of guilt necessitates a distinction of self from others, an awareness of one's actions toward others, and understanding of one's own choices and responsibilities ("attribution" is a psychological term referring to one's inferences concerning causality; the need to posit attributions appears intrinsic for everyday human functioning).

Paradoxically, Hoffman notes that guilt, albeit really the result of non-prosocial action, in turn leads one to act prosocially. Further, the separateness between empathic distress (observing the hurt of the other) and guilt (perpetrating an action injurious to the other) requires close scrutiny.

> The line between empathic distress and guilt thus becomes very fine, and being an innocent bystander is a matter of degree. To the degree that one realizes that one could have acted to help but did not, one may never feel totally innocent. This is another way of saying that empathy and guilt may be the quintessential social motives, because they may transform another's pain into one's own discomfort and make one feel partly responsible for the other's plight whether or not one has actually done anything to cause it.[62]

Empathy: Altruistic or Egoistic?

Hoffman appears particularly concerned about the charge that relieving empathic distress through prosocial responding is actually more in line with egoistic than altruistic motivation. For one, even though showing care to another might reduce empathic distress, the aim of the prosocial act is the aid of the distressed person. Hoffman maintains that critics fail to distinguish between the consequence and the aim of an action. Second, when individuals, including children, are questioned about their aid of distressed others, they answer in terms of the other's plight rather than their own distress. Third, although some theorists suggest that individuals perform caring acts for self-reward, Hoffman argues that it is neither likely that the misery of others would engender self-reward nor that satisfying self-reward would be dependent upon helping someone in distress. This is the case because "there is nothing intrinsically prosocial about self-reward, as there is about empathy."[63] Furthermore, self-reward is too contingent upon cultural factors and too variable to serve as an evolutionary criterion for an altruistic human nature. Fourth, sympathetic distress is aroused by hurt experienced by the other rather than distress arising from one's own personal experience. Fifth, gratification for helping the other depends on the alleviation of the other's plight, rather than focusing on one's own welfare. And lastly, all motives have the potential for satisfying the person; as this is the case, such satisfaction cannot be used to define a distinctive class of motives (e.g., altruistic or egoistic motives). Furthermore, such an inclusive interpretation renders as useless the very idea of altruism.

Hoffman does appear to be walking a difficult trail in his attempt to establish an independent altruistic motive. On the one hand, he appears to accept the satisfaction that goes with all human actions. On the other hand, he wishes to establish the viable nature of an altruistic response. In sum, Hoffman appears to recognize the satisfaction that prosocial actions have for the person, yet he maintains that empathic responding serves as a distinctively prosocial action that supports the view of an altruistic human nature. Thus,

> it is more appropriate to designate empathic distress as an altruistic motive (perhaps, with a quasi-egoistic component) than to group it with such obviously self-serving motives as material gain, social approval, and competitive success.[64]

Can One Be Too Empathic?

If empathy is integral to the formation of altruism, then a legitimate question arises regarding the degree of one's empathic arousal. Does there exist a perfect relationship between empathy and care? That is, as one is more empathically aroused by a situation, is one also more caring and prosocially inclined? Hoffman believes one must look at the level of one's empathic experience. Too little arousal at the distress of another lessens sympathetic distress (compassion). Equally important, however, empathic overarousal impedes caring. Studies indicate that when one's empathic experience is too intense, there exists a tendency to disengage from another. In effect, overly distressed individuals become self-absorbed, with a need to attend to their own difficult state, thereby inhibiting the ability to attend to the needs of others. Interestingly, Hoffman speculates that the lack of relationship between empathic overarousal and helping others aided evolutionary survival; that is, overarousal is often associated with severe if not hopeless situations that enable the observer, therefore, to conserve energies and interventions for more hopeful helping situations.

The presence of empathic overarousal, moreover, is a likely explanation for why burnout is so prominent among people in highly stressed caring professions. Emergency health care workers, mental health professionals, and those engaged in ministry are continually confronted by difficult and highly charged situations that tax emotional and physical resources. Often these instances produce a high degree of empathic feelings. Over time, the stress of such overarousal can lead to burnout and an inability to really be present or show care for another.

In a similar vein, those who are engaged in work for social justice are also vulnerable to this phenomenon. When confronting stark injustice and the suffering and powerlessness of others, one's empathic feelings are continually exposed, which, with time, can lead to frustration, hardened feelings, bitterness, and burnout. This phenomenon is particularly likely when the minister is confronted with impervious social structures and feels a sense of powerlessness in eradicating them. The experience of helplessness, in other words, contributes to ongoing empathic distress. Psychologically, it is inevitable that one's physical/emotional capacities "shut down." In order to counter these experiences, it is imperative that ministers and health care workers have support groups or viable communities and periodic rest (what might be termed "buffer" experiences). Another helpful antidote is periodic reflection on one's own values and commitments that provide a rationale and purposive foundation for one's behavior, particularly when facing stressful situations.

In a related fashion, just as one can experience empathic overarousal, so too can one exhibit what is best termed compulsive care giving. One can become an addicted care giver. Such individuals are characterized by an obsessive desire to "do" for others, but lack the capacity to allow others to "do" for them, or for that matter they often find it difficult simply to "be" with another. Mature interpersonal relationships with such individuals are invariably compromised by their inability to experience reliance on the other and express their own vulnerabilities.

Sex Differences in Empathy

If empathy is a foundational experience for morality, then investigation of possible gender differences is appropriate. Clearly, the presence of sex differences poses ethical and philosophical problems for an empathically based morality; in short, such inequality relegates the disadvantaged sex to a condition of moral inferiority.

Early reviews of the literature established the belief that there existed clear sex differences regarding empathy. By all accounts it appeared that females were more empathically inclined than males.[65]

More recently, psychologists Nancy Eisenberg and Randy Lennon have undertaken an exhaustive analysis of the extant literature in order to ascertain whether sex differences in empathy do indeed exist. These psychologists employed meta-analytic techniques (statistical manipulations that allow one to examine a wide variety of studies). They noted there exist a wide variety of techniques used to study empathy. These include reflexes, picture/story instruments; self-reports (subjects simply respond to questionnaires); physiological measures; analysis of facial, vocal, and gestural features.[66]

All in all, Eisenberg and Lennon conclude that gender differences regarding empathy are a function of the methodology employed. In other words, whether empathic experiences between males and females are reported is dependent upon the instrument used for measurement as well as the methods used to carry out the experiment. Use of self-report measures most consistently show sex differences, but such self-presentations (responses to questionnaires) are explained by influences such as cultural stereotypes and societal expectations. That is, when differences do exist between the sexes, there exists the distinct possibility that such differences are the product of upbringing. Females, in other words, "learn" to be more empathic through socialization to a female role that values care and sensitivity whereas the male learns to be more assertive and action-oriented. Consequently, empathic expression is more encouraged in females than males.

Thus, the overwhelming conclusion that can be drawn from self-report measures is that there exists a clear difference between the capacity of males and females for empathy. Interpretation of such findings, however, warrants close and critical scrutiny. In sum, Eisenberg and Lennon state that any conclusions drawn from the extant empirical research must be "circumscribed and tentative." They conclude that "indeed, at the present, all that can be concluded with confidence is that many important issues concerning sex differences in emotional empathy are, as yet, unresolved."[67] Thus, whether "real" differences do indeed exist is a question the research has yet to answer. A more recent examination of studies carried out over the past few years supports this conclusion. "The review of recent research concerning gender differences in empathy does not alter the conclusion of our 1983 review, namely, that gender differences in empathy may be an artifact of the method of measurement."[68]

Problems with an Empathic Morality

Though we have argued for a morality of care with empathy as its basis, the complexity of situations, not to mention the diverse perspectives from which morality can be approached, raises issues regarding the adequacy of an empathic morality. Some of these issues are discussed below.

Empathic Bias

Hoffman has pointed out that empathy might lead one to overly stress some individuals and groups, thereby leading to lack of awareness of others who are in need, or even a bias against them.[69]

Justice Issues

There exist issues for which empathy does not provide a guiding perspective on the resolution of the problem. For example, a mayor of a city might have only limited funds and have pressing concerns for several programs, all crucially important, and all deserving the maximum level of funding. The limitation of funds might, however, preclude all groups from receiving such funding. What is just in such situations? Empathy cannot provide a clear response. Numerous other examples exist. A company is facing severe financial losses. As a way to reduce costs, the union agrees to a policy whereby workers work one of two one-month shifts. While the one shift is working, the other remains idle. Such a policy runs contrary to seniority rules that guarantee a full work week for senior employees. On the other hand, it insures that younger workers are not laid off. Consequently, most older workers oppose the plan whereas younger workers endorse it. Is it moral that senior workers should remain idle? Another example: A large utility company wishes to lay a cable that will provide service. The cable is most cheaply laid by going through farm land and disrupting the lives of hundreds of farmers over several thousand miles. The farmers oppose such a policy. What is the moral response? Empathy-based morality is clearly limited in such situations. The context of these situations requires, then, discussion of other ethical principles and philosophical perspectives.

Institutional Issues

Whereas one might feel empathically disposed to a certain situation that orients one to a personal response, a more broadly based institutional action might be warranted. An empathic morality, for example, might be vulnerable to the needs of unemployed workers and lead one to expend resources directly for them. But a more productive response might be to channel funding through a governmental structure that is more capable of providing services and arriving at a long-term solution.

Questions of Personal Goodness

Because empathy is focused on the other it has difficulty addressing questions that strike at more personal issues such as one's view of and care for the self. In this regard, the question of adolescent suicide comes to mind. Mature moral functioning requires a healthy sense of self-esteem and a sense of "inner goodness"; otherwise, one is prey to "needy" responses or attempts that, on the surface are believed to be moral, yet are more apt to be performed to fill up a felt inner void.

Directional Focus

Empathy provides a general direction oriented toward care. Obviously, empathic arousal is disposed toward values such as compassion and love and might even exercise a role in articulating fairness. Yet one could conceivably wallow in one's empathic response with no clear directional focus. As Hogan notes, empathy "can produce an equivocating jellyfish as well as a compassionate person with a broad moral perspective."[70]

Though these issues exist, empathy can be of service even with the limitations stated above. Strategies can be employed to deal with empathic bias. Even though questions of justice are significant in their own right and are the salient issue in some moral discussions, empathy as Hoffman points out, can be utilized to uphold or induce one to consider issues of fairness.[71] For example, one's empathy would serve as a focal point for leading to awareness of another's situation, which could then further the desire for equality or equity. Even though social institutions and administrative decision makers might not consider an empathic reaction the more helpful response, the experience of empathy helps decision makers shed a cold and hardened approach to serious ocial problems. Without empathy, decision makers are all too prone to adopt an unreflective efficiency and calculated pragmatism.

What we point to here is the inevitable tendency for *habituation*. Humans are creatures of habit and, with time, sensitivity is sacrificed for efficiency and simplicity. Above all, though, empathy forces to consciousness the issue of personal suffering, which is often inevitable in any distribution of goods. Though empathy does not directly speak to questions of "personal goodness," the amelioration of problems associated with personal goodness issues (e.g., low self-esteem, self-hate, suicidal behaviors), cannot be addressed adequately unless empathic expressions, which are essential for interpersonal functioning and sound mental health, are forthcoming.

Finally, questions of a directional focus are aided by empathy, which is apt to further awareness of the priority of love as well as induce the raising of the fairness principle (through, for example, the experience of "empathic anger" directed toward the person causing an injustice).

Moreover, the presence of some evaluative stance (ideology, value reference) is likely to direct one's empathic expression for two reasons. For one, it gives meaning to one's empathic arousal as well as guidelines as to the degree to which one can be empathic. For example, one can have a set of beliefs about parenting ("being a good parent") that leads one to empathize with the struggles of one's child. Yet belief in self-reliance and the need at times to "let go" might temper such empathic experience when one's child faces failure, for the parent realizes the need for the child to face such struggles alone. Second, a set of deeply held beliefs can orient one to certain situations and experiences that in turn foster empathy. Thus, an individual considering himself or herself Christian might be more sensitive to reading about certain issues or perceiving specific situations that foster empathic experiences. No doubt this process is mutually reinforcing inasmuch as empathy sustains one's values and beliefs.

In this chapter we have considered the vital role empathy exercises in forming caring responses. We have maintained that empathy is a constitutive element of human experience and can be the basis for a morality whose focus is care. Moreover, though other moral issues such as justice most certainly exist, the fundamental experience of being human is tied to empathic expression, an experience that emerges at the earliest stages of life. This core experience is at the "heart" of the moral life, and it is to this metaphor that we now turn to show the essence of the moral life.

> *Chapter 4* ≺

Toward a Morality of the Heart

On the scales of God, only hearts have any weight.
—Karl Rahner

In our second chapter we viewed the role of reason in forming a justice ethic. We do not want to dismiss by any means the critical importance of rules and impartiality that Kohlberg's approach champions; yet taken by itself it is an inadequate representation of morality. More to the point, there are many instances of moral growth that Kohlberg's moral psychology is unable to account for. Why is this so? We listed several criticisms of Kohlberg's approach. All of these criticisms of Kohlberg's view of morality can best be summed up by the word "ahistorical." Stated simply, Kohlberg's approach is unable to appreciate fully the life history and complexity of the human person. It is unable to account for vital aspects of human living that have shaped who we are and that are essential for understanding our selves as moral persons.

What are these vital ingredients that are lacking in Kohlberg's account? A hint to answering this question was provided in chapter 3 when we explored the role of empathy and the moral life. Given the limitations of Kohlberg's approach we reflected on the significance of an empathically based morality. More specifically, an empathic morality is oriented toward an understanding of the other's life situation. Through the interplay of empathy's cognitive and affective components one is drawn to an essential bondedness with another. Furthermore, the very experience of empathy frames one's life in a directional focus, orienting one to caring responses closely allied with loving self-sacrifice. Though the experience of empathy does not guarantee an expression of love, most certainly love itself would be impossible without a developed empathic capacity. Moreover, as defined in Martin Hoffman's conceptual schema, empathy emerges as a catalyst for altruistic action. More broadly, the focus on empathy points to the significance of relationships and bonding. It points out that being a moral person means not only being someone who understands, but also someone who *feels*, and that this experience must be accorded significant weight when coming to understand the moral life. The role of sensitivity, likewise, must be fostered in any discussion of morality. How are we morally responsive to the needs of others? Finally, there exists the need for a moral vision. Where do our desires lead us? Who are we becoming? Who do we desire to be? Philosopher Lawrence Hinman captures both the strength and weakness of Kohlberg's approach when he notes:

> I certainly do not want to argue that the standard view of morality is completely wrong. Clearly it captures something important about the moral life, namely, that it is in part constituted by rules, impartiality, and specific choices. Yet at the same time, it is equally clear that it leaves out an important aspect of the moral life, namely the development of character, moral sensitivity, and vision.[1]

He goes on to say:

> Precisely because of the stress which it places on the impartial application of moral principles and on the importance of choices made largely in isolation from questions of individual character, Kohlberg's approach puts far too little emphasis on the cultivation of the moral emotions, the sharpening of moral perceptions, and the development of moral sensitivity.[2]

Given our questioning of Kohlberg's moral psychology, how might we envision a moral view that encompasses the empathically based morality we propose? What metaphor might capture the psychological dynamics of empathy as it is reflected in a morality of care as well as the vision, sensitivity, and character we view as essential for the moral life? I propose that the metaphor of "heart" best captures the moral perspective we wish to set forth.

The Meaning of "Heart"

Pascal's famous dictum comes to mind: "The heart has its reasons, which reason does not know." This uniqueness of the heart is best represented through aspiration and emotion. That is, "the 'heart' refers to the agent as engaged, as a being of vision and feeling. In biblical morality it is the seat of affectivity and virtuous qualities."[3]

Hans Walter Wolff notes that "the most important word in the vocabulary of Hebrew Bible anthropology is generally translated 'heart.'"[4] It occurs 858 times in the Hebrew Bible. In the Hebrew Bible, the "heart" takes on a variety of meanings. Heart is expressed as the depth of one's desires, the source for feelings and temperament, the catalyst for understanding and insight, the origin of ethical judgment, and as the description of one's very self. In all these interpretable frames, the heart surfaces as the essential aspect of personhood.[5]

Karl Rahner captures most profoundly the nature of the word "heart."[6] Rahner notes that the word "heart" is an *Urwort*, what is best translated as a source or primordial word. An *Urwort* is rooted in multiple understandings and numerous layers of meaning. Such words are highly evocative, threaded with nuances and pregnant with inexhaustible depth. What is central for Rahner is the capacity for the "heart" to define at the most fundamental level one's very personhood. "Heart," for Rahner, portrays the core experience of who we are as human beings. We quote Rahner at length to capture the essence of this primordial word:

> So long as man has a heart, he will have to speak of it with this precise word "heart." That is to say, always. He will always speak of the heart, whenever at once simple and wise he recalls himself from multiplicity to his one source. Always, whenever he gathers the permanent essence of his time into the eternity of his existence he will say that he has stored it in the storing-place of his heart. Always, when he renounces himself completely and utterly, he will say, "I give you my heart." Always, when he plunges down into the dark abyss of his being, it will seem to him that he is caught in the dungeons of his dead and empty heart. Always, he will sing simply, "Go out my heart and seek for joy!" Always, he will glorify his restoration to grace as an outpouring of the Holy Spirit into his heart. Always, he who is slandered will comfort himself with the fact that God sees his heart. Always, men will hope that "the morning-star will rise in the heart," always call those blessed who are pure of heart, always experience horror at evil gushing up out of the quarry of the heart, and always be happy that goodness can be preserved in the heart, always love those who are able to forgive from the heart, always be

judged by this alone, whether they have loved with their whole heart, because on the scales of God only hearts have any weight.[7]

Relatedly, Rahner points to the essential nature of "heart's" linkage to humankind when he writes:

Heart as a total-human primordial word of this kind denotes the core of the human person which is original and inmost with respect to everything else in the human person, in which the whole concrete "being of man, as it is brought forth and unfolded and flows away in soul, body and spirit... is taken and grasped (and remains) as one, as though knotted and fastened at its mid-point" (H. Conrad-Martius), at which therefore man is originally and wholly related to other persons and above all also to God, who is interested in the person as a whole and whose action in giving grace or guidance is therefore aimed at this heart-centre of man.[8]

Rahner's reflections display the heart's power for relational bondedness as well as for a human existence rooted in care. Further, heart distills the core meaning of personhood for it portrays one's most authentic desires (that which is most true of one's very nature qua person) as tied to a sense of loving care for another. Rahner's theologically oriented speculations on "heart" blend nicely with Hoffman's psychology of human nature, which posits the universal experience of empathy as a basis for naturally occurring altruistic expressions.

As a way to test the evocative power of the word "heart," I conducted a study in my introductory psychology classes. I asked my students two questions. First: "You are talking with a close friend about a certain person. Your friend says to you that the person you are discussing 'really has a heart.' How would you interpret your friend's statement? That is, what do you think the phrase 'really has a heart' means when you say it about someone?" The responses among nearly one hundred students were unanimous. Every student, when describing such a person, used adjectives and descriptions associated with care. A brief sample will suffice. One student stated that such a person "understands what others are going through." Another stated: such a person "puts him or herself in others' shoes." Other descriptions included words such as "unselfish," "friendliness," "sacrificing," "loving and giving," "caring," and one who "listens." These expressions point to a fundamental empathic sensitivity oriented toward care for another.

I then asked my students the following question: "If this person who 'really has a heart' did something that hurt someone, how do you think this person would feel? What would he or she do?"

The results were, again, unanimous and similar to Hoffman's psychological description about guilt and its power to move one to respond in a caring manner. Feelings the students associated with such a person included "feeling bad," "miserable," "guilty," "awful," "ashamed." Further, the responses characterizing this imagined person were highly altruistic, that is, focused on aiding the other and making restitution. A sample of student responses includes "do something to make amends," "help the other," "make up for what happened," "go out of one's way to help the person."

The results of this short survey demonstrate both that 'heart' is understood to mean caring as well as the fact that empathy is inextricably tied to the "heart" and is best expressed by this word. As noted, it does not exhaust the meaning of heart for, as an *Urwort*, such finality is impossible. Yet the experience of empathic distress touches one at a core level of human meaning. It arouses one to experience the fundamental bonding we have as humans. Further it orients us to reach out in caring sensitivity. Its power can provide one with a unity not only with whom one loves, but, as Hoffman rightly points out, in its highly developed form with entire classes, groups, races (what we have termed in the preceding chapter as "existential solidarity"). In a similar vein, psychologist Kenneth Clark notes

the highest and probably the least frequent form of empathy is that in which the individual is compelled to embrace all human beings. This expanded empathy is the most difficult level to achieve. It probably requires the highest level of development of the anterior frontal lobe of the brain, reinforced by training and experience. It is a level of empathy that can be simulated by verbal adherence but remains most difficult to express consistently and functionally. It is the level of empathy that religion seeks to reinforce, with varying degrees of failure. It is the level of empathy that is neglected by those practical and self-defined objective educators and social scientists who substitute moral relativism for moral sensitivity in propagating their trade. It is a level of empathy that intellectuals frequently seek to rationalize by obfuscating contemplations of the impossibility of verifying empirical ethics. It is the level of empathy that when real and functional can not be used to justify the naked use of power, tyranny, flagrant or subtle injustices, cruelties, sustained terrorism, killings, wars, and eventual distinction.[9]

The fullest meaning of the word "heart" is captured in the above expression by psychologist Kenneth Clark's reflection on developed empathy. From a psychological perspective, it is the "heart" energized by empathic stirrings that acts compassionately, that reaches out even when there is hurt, and that perseveres in self-sacrificing ways, even in the midst of seemingly insurmountable odds.

From another perspective, labeling someone as having a "heart" helps to define the perennial question, "Who is a moral person?" One can think of a person with limited education and few resources. Yet in the midst of the trials and stress of life, this person responds compassionately to others. He or she is available to others and reaches out to them. The tribulations of everyday life do not deter such a person from displaying caring sensitivity. Even though his or her life is often mundane and he or she cannot provide articulate and reasoned answers for "why" his or her actions take place, none of us would label this person as anything but "moral." We would use terms such as "(s)he is a really good person." Such a person has a "heart of gold." Around such people we feel secure and know we will not be taken advantage of. Fortunately, we all know such people.

Most men, however, seem to know just what human goodness is when they see it, whether they have read treatises on morality or not, or whether or not they have tried to fathom its meta-physical foundations. For the fact is, it seems to have no such foundations, and no treatises on morals or disquisitions on the nature of true justice make it stand forth with more clarity than it already has. It would be as odd to suppose that one must become a philosopher before he can hope to recognize genuine moral good and evil, as it would to suppose that no man can be overwhelmed by a sunset until he understands the physics of refraction.[10]

What accounts, psychologically, for this almost effortless intuition that leads us to utter and point to some women and men as "moral." Indeed, to view them as unfailing guides and sources of inspiration in the midst of our own moral struggles? It is our own empathic experiences that allow such statements to flow so effortlessly and be believed with such certainty. Empathic experiencing is our kinship with all humanity. Empathy is foundational soil, psychologically, for our rooting in the moral life. Perceiving another's altruistic actions triggers one's own empathic stirrings as well as pivotal life events that are empathically arousing, all of which help to sculpt our moral lives.

I will never forget, for example, the mother of two classmates that I knew in a small southern Illinois town where I attended grade school for several years. Her intelligence was limited (what I have now come to see as borderline intellectual functioning). She was a single parent struggling both emotionally and financially to raise two children. She worked in a menial job, yet there was something enduringly noble about her. She made sure her son and daughter attended school and did their homework. Though poor, she always volunteered to make cookies at the school fair. She faithfully attended PTA meetings and was at every school function, even though she did not always comprehend everything going on. Moreover, she shared whatever she had with others and instilled such desires in her children.

Even though I did not know this woman well (and today I cannot even remember her name), her life and commitment to her children are indelibly etched in my consciousness and have become a powerful model for my own life. Her goodness was unquestionable; her heart profound. Whenever I think of her I cannot help but feel morally energized and desirous to do good, even though my own actions often do not follow through in this regard. When imagining her I am able to feel my own vulnerability and frailty as I empathize with her. These empathic recollections trigger within me a conscious experience of my own value orientation and what enduring principles are central for my own moral quest. At times, these empathic reflections stir me to evaluate my own moral life. How do I compare with this woman? What must my own heart do to resemble hers? In turn, such recollections engender other empathic experiences where care and love are significant for my life.

From a similar perspective, the images nourished by empathic experience need not be focused on positive moral memories (recollections that provide role modeling and the desire to emulate another). One can empathize with those whom we have hurt and injured. The visualization of another's pain or their distress arising from our own actions provides another catalyst for our moral lives. The evoking of such memories and the awareness of such painful experiences prove compelling for shaping our current and future moral actions. A close friend recounted to me a painful experience from his own childhood. In his very early years he lived with his parents and an elderly aunt. One day his aunt accidently stepped on the family dog. The dog's whine led the young child, who did not quite understand what was going on, to point to the aunt as the culprit, thereupon leading the mother to react in a somewhat scolding manner toward the aunt. The pain on the aunt's face at her unintended misstep with the dog was obvious. What was so painful for my friend, though, was the empathy he had for his aunt and the accompanying guilt he bore as he realized his role in causing her pain by innocently stating what his aunt had done. Since this very early incident in his life, my friend continues to make reference to this experience and his feelings for his aunt as a reminder of his own moral frailty and a reference point as to his need to respond lovingly to others.[11] In sum, memories of relationships with parents, significant others, colleagues, or even acquaintances who stir us empathically serve to sustain our hearts.

How can such simple memories be so empowering? Why do they become so pivotal for us in our own quest for moral identity? Again, we are psychologically oriented to respond empathically to others; certain events touch our empathic stirrings and engender compassionate desires within (Hoffman's sympathetic distress). Even uneventful and less than significant events have the power to prove nobly enduring.

> From the standpoint of the good of the world as a whole, they are almost devoid of significance. Yet, one stands in a certain awe of them all, as soon as he sees what lies behind them; it is a compassionate heart that manages to overcome fear, hatred, and the sense of duty itself. However little it has won the praise of moralists and theologians, however little it may deck itself out with the ornamentation of intellect and reason, however strange and mysterious it may seem to the mind, it is still the fugitive and unpredictable thing that alone quickens moral esteem and stamps its possessor as a man who, although fallible and ignorant and capable of much evil, is nevertheless a man of deep goodness and virtue.[12]

From where does the compassionate heart derive its power? What is the glue that cements the union of empathic stirring and the heart's desire for compassionate responding? It is the experience of emotion that provides such power, and it is to this experience that we now turn.

The Psychology of Emotion and Our Moral Lives

Though the cognitive view of morality (best demonstrated by Kohlberg's emphasis on impartiality and moral reasoning) has remained dominant, it is fair to say there exists an affective basis for morality encompassing the empathically based foundation we have set forth. This alternative view of morality stresses the role of emotion and resonates with the focus on moral sensitivity, character, virtue, and moral vision.

Why does an affective basis for morality always receive less emphasis? Several reasons exist for this phenomenon. First, the emotions are usually viewed as irrational. Among academics, particularly philosophers, there exists a bias toward rational reflection. In essence, only the rational is perceived as capable of truth.

A second reason rests with what is often termed the dark side of human nature:

> one reason many scholars have preferred to base morality on logic, rather than on feeling, is that most Western philosophers have assumed human nature to be basically selfish, cruel, and deceitful. As a result, they could not trust a person's emotion as a basis for ethical choice and had to insert the idea of will between a person's strong desire and his behavior.[13]

In this regard, the work of Hoffman goes a long way in gainsaying this implicit premise of accepting only a dark side to human nature. Accepting altruism as a naturally occurring response points to human nature as capable of nobly enduring acts.

In addition, many philosophers would hold that only the rational is capable of providing a universal context for morality. In short, rational men and women everywhere can reason to the same ends, that is, the same view of justice (as Kohlberg continually points out). This consensus appears beyond the power of a more emotion-based view of morality. The expression of various emotions is highly conditioned by the culture; hence the ever present threat of relativism exists.

Another reason for the primacy of reason in moral discourse is that emotions are believed to lack an evaluative dimension. In other words, in order to come to an understanding of right and wrong, emotions add little to the moral discussion.

> By insisting on the rational justification of a moral principle, philosophers hoped to make it possible to judge a moral standard as correct or incorrect. Such an evaluation cannot be applied when feelings are the basis for judging moral ideas.[14]

Yet examination of the cognitive perspective leaves many questions. In effect, there exist several meanings for "cognition" that deserve scrutiny. First, there is the cognitive-developmental perspective of Kohlberg. Second, cognition can refer to the processing of information that enables one to arrive at a decision. Finally, cognition can mean one's interpretation and understanding of a situation (Hoffman's usage). A careful reading of the cognitive argument for morality, particularly as it has been sketched by Kohlberg, has been evaluated critically in chapter 2. In addition, though, there are several risks related to the reasoning one might employ as well as to the process one utilizes to come to a decision.

First, theorists can formulate arguments that invariably lead to diverse and contradictory conclusions. Almost any question of ethics today is expressed in a variety of rational arguments that are often at variance and in conflict. Rational reflection appears to provide no sure proof or resolution to the multitudinous ethical questions that exist today. No one rational position enjoys universal consensus, for many ethical positions are persuasive.

Second, the reasoning behind why certain intellectual pursuits are chosen or rational arguments are presented is often far from rational. Sophisticated reasoning can mask a variety of unconscious motivations. A classic example of this is pointed out by psychiatrist Ben-Ami Scharfstein, who speculates on how much of the philosopher Nietzsche's thinking was grounded in unresolved issues with his father.[15] To take another example, a professor who has a psychological need for control rationalizes that a student's dissertation is deficient; that is, he objects to the scholarly study because of academic deficiencies yet has, on an unconscious level, the need to feel powerful and hold others in a position of dependence. These unconscious motivations do not make one's rational arguments wrong, yet they do lead one to approach them critically inasmuch as their articulation arises not so much from scholarly purpose and the search for truth but from unconscious motivations.

A final argument showing the limits of cognition is simply that our everyday reasoning is itself subject to numerous processing errors. An information processing approach to psychology has documented this. Information processing focuses on the human organism's capacity to receive, transform, and express information. It emphasizes the various mental processes utilized in interpreting information that humans receive from the environment. In an information processing approach, mental operations are often compared to those of a computer. I would like to document a few of the most commonplace errors in cognitive processing that can lead one to make false premises and render one's conclusions suspect.[16]

For one, when we have a view of how something is, we tend to interpret information in ways that support our original premises. This is known as the law of overinterpretation (in effect we simplify incoming information and are predisposed to accept data that support our original hypotheses). Naturally, our reasoning invariably strives to be efficient and to narrow our interpretations of life around that which is consonant with our way of viewing and believing. To accept too much contradictory information strains cognitive functioning.

Other research has indicated that positive mental health is associated with the capacity to distort reality. We tend not to believe what is really happening for fear of its effects on our tacit assumptions about self and the world. Well functioning people, in other words, do not confront reality in toto; rather, they selectively perceive life events and interpret the world in ways that enhance their own well being. In this regard, the research has noted that:

> the mentally healthy person may not be fully cognizant of the day-to-day flotsam and jetsam of life. Rather, the mentally healthy person appears to have the enviable capacity to distort reality in a direction that enhances self-esteem, maintains beliefs in personal efficacy and promotes an optimistic view of the future. These three illusions, as we have called them, appear to foster traditional criteria of mental health, including the ability to care about the self and others, the ability to be happy or contented, and the ability to engage in productive and creative work.[17]

In effect, humans possess a remarkable distorting power that is continually employed to avoid disruptive thoughts and negative self-evaluations.

Another cognitive error often found in our reasoning is that of "self-serving bias." We are apt to value information that enhances our self-esteem or support information that indirectly reflects well on our own efforts. Still another cognitive error often experienced is that of "availability." Each of us has worked out attributions (causes) for various life events. In short, we are familiar with information that sustains our underlying premises about life. We are familiar with such information and the numerous arguments employed (availability) and are apt to dismiss arguments that differ from our tacitly accepted assumptions. In other words, we have a pool of arguments and reasons we draw upon and these are readily available to us. Thus, interpretations of causes of events or sources of information at variance with our own causal attributions are dismissed. Consequently, we "may overestimate the validity of particular causal beliefs due, in part, to their inability to generate arguments opposing those beliefs."[18]

These criticisms of cognitive processing do not by any means downgrade cognition's significant contribution in making moral decisions. Recall that even Hoffman's theory provides a vital role for cognition. Moreover, rational reflection is an absolutely *necessary* part of moral decision making and becomes all the more urgent as ethical decisions involve multiple values and complex issues. Furthermore, emotions themselves have the power for profound distortion. The essence of psychoanalytic theory is the ego's need to protect itself from diminished self-esteem and to enhance its own functioning. As Norma Haan has pointed out, individuals go to enormous lengths to view themselves as moral. "The impetus for Freud's theory of the ego defenses was his understanding that people engage in all manner of self and social deception to avoid feeling immoral."[19]

As a consequence, there exist numerous defense mechanisms whose sole purpose is to protect the ego's need to maintain a sense of moral goodness. Emotions such as anger, guilt, and shame, though having the power to engender noble action, also have the capability to disrupt seriously one's sense of moral adequacy. Defense mechanisms are employed by the ego to ward off anxiety and feelings that threaten self-esteem.[20] There exists a large number of defenses. Some defenses, however, aid one to maintain falsely a sense of moral goodness. These defenses are discussed briefly below.[21]

Minimization. Minimization is utilized when one downplays an issue. For example, a worker dismisses the importance of an assignment he failed to finish on time, thereby enabling him or her to avoid the feeling of inadequacy.

Denial. To protect one's feeling of adequacy, an individual unconsciously refuses to recognize new facts that cast doubt on that person's self-image. A parent fails to consider evidence that shows limited ability in his or her child. This might be done because of a parental need to view the child as someone very special, which then serves to augment the parent's fragile self-esteem.

Distortion. This defense mechanism is activated by a person's altering of the reality at hand. A club member distorts what went on at a meeting because of unconscious resentment toward the president of the club who chaired the meeting.

Rationalization. Rationalization is a very commonly employed defense mechanism. Simply stated, we rationalize when we make excuses for our actions.

Externalization. When we externalize we blame someone else for our own failures. The adolescent who does poorly on a test blames the teacher for not explaining the material adequately.

Inhibition. The inhibited person is one who is unable to take action when necessary.

Acting Out. The opposite of inhibition is acting out. This defense mechanism results when one is unable to control or suppress inappropriate behavior. Often when one acts out one is attempting to cope with some internally conflicted state. Another problem with acting out is that it limits the reflection so essential for the moral life.

Compartmentalization. We compartmentalize when we selectively look at areas of our lives and fail to scrutinize our actions regarding other areas. One of the most commonplace examples of this phenomenon is the person who lives a "good" life but is blind to examining one or another area of life (e.g., morally questionable sexual expression).

Idealization. When we view others or ourselves in an overly positive light we are utilizing the defense of idealization. It should be noted that a "healthy" sense of idealization (not a defense mechanism) comes into play when we experience healthy ideals, dreams, desires. Idealization as a defense mechanism arises from distorting one's self or another's positive qualities.

Stereotyping. Failure to view the complexity or ambiguity of people or situations leads one to form stereotypes. This defense prevents one from viewing equivocal, enigmatic, and uncertain life events that often prove the catalyst for moral growth.

In sum, defense mechanisms provide a vital function for everyday psychic functioning. They enable one to maintain a fundamental sense of moral integrity when confronted with the reality of human frailty. In themselves, defense mechanisms provide a vital psychological function inasmuch as they prevent the ego from being overwhelmed. This functioning becomes, however, a double-edged sword when it renders one oblivious to actual transgressions. In essence, they prevent self-scrutiny and moral growth.

Nonetheless, emotions have been given far too little credit in discussions of the moral life. Emotions serve as a vital if not the central ingredient in sculpting moral identity.

Emotions are best defined as subjective experiences of varying intensity that orient us to an action-ready state of responding.[22] Psychologists have been able to identify various structures of the emotions.[23] These are physiological, expressive, and experiential. The physiological structures are neural pathways that trigger emotional arousal. The central nervous system appears to be structurally wired for emotional responding. Part of this response (subcortical) appears independent of cognition.

A well-documented debate in psychology today is the question as to whether emotions, to exist, must be preceded by some type of cognitive activity. A growing body of research demonstrates that emotions can be experienced independent of cognition. In other words, human behavior appears capable of emotional response that is prior to any cognitive evaluation of a situation or event. There appears to be what might be termed a "primacy of affect"; we feel before we actually think (interpret stimuli and become aware of the situation).[24] Thus some researchers believe that there need not be cognitive processing in order to respond emotionally. Some evidence supports this position. There exist neural circuits not involving cognition. It might well be that some very simple processes such as fear of an animal might involve little if any cognitive activity.[25] On the other hand, more complex emotional experiences (e.g., anger, love) involve the complex interplay of emotional and cognitive processes.

Moreover, there exist neural pathways that are interlocked with cognitive processing that form the basis for activating emotional responses. Carroll Izard has been among the most influential psychologists in this area and his work documents both the independence of emotional arousal as well as the interlocking nature of cognition and affect:

> Recent research in neuroscience and developmental psychology...suggests there may be two circuits of neural pathways that activate emotions — one automatic and subconscious, activated through the subcortical pathway, and one mediated by cognition and relayed from the thalamus to the amygdala and neocortex. Once cognitive capacities have developed, both neural-evaluative processes probably go to work simultaneously...with the subcortical pathway providing the initial emotion response and the corticolimbic pathway providing an adjusted response based on perceptual organization, discrimination, comparison and appraisal.[26]

The expressive function of emotion is viewed through various "facial, vocal, postural, and gestural expressions."[27] The experiential component of emotion is the subjective experience of emotion that in essence is the conscious experience of one's own emotional state. According to Izard, our subjective experience "is the aspect of emotion that acquires consciousness."[28]

The Contribution of Emotion to the Moral Life

One of the most stimulating theories in recent developmental research is viewing morality as originating in the experience of emotion rather than cognition (our understandings and interpretations of the world). The most eloquent spokesperson for this position is Harvard psychologist Robert Kagan.

Kagan begins by posing the question as to whether there can be universal standards. Moral philosophy answers no because of the cultural differences existing among various groups. In other words, what is considered a valued ideal in Western Europe would often be at variance with the values prized by tribal custom in a third world country (e.g., the question of individual freedom regarding the choice of a marriage partner). Further, moral acts themselves are dependent on the context: interpreting any situation is dependent on cultural mores and customs. The consequence of such thinking is the predominance of moral relativism.

In contrast to this state of affairs, Kagan proposes a linkage between universal standards and emotion:

> I believe, however, that, beneath the extraordinary variety in surface behavior and consciously articulated ideals, there is a set of emotional states that form the bases for a limited number of universal moral categories that transcend time and locality. . . . The human competence to experience a small number of distinctive emotional states can be likened to the preservation of basic morphological structures in evolution — the eye is an example — each of which is expressed in varied phenotypes but descended from an original, fundamental form.[29]

Each society, says Kagan, has a list of virtues it endorses.

> The virtues awarded the highest praise during any historical period will require effort but will be within the capacity of all citizens. Assume further that the virtues easiest to promote in others, and to defend to oneself, are those that prevent the unpleasant feelings accompanying temptations to violate a standard, that mute the discomfort following a violation, and that generate pleasant emotions through practice of the virtue.[30]

Violations of various standards lead to unpleasant feelings whereas upholding virtues allows for feelings that are pleasant in nature. All in all,

> the unpleasant emotions are provoked by specific conditions that occur with different probabilities across communities. Five potential candidates are: anticipation of the different varieties of "anxiety" in response to possible physical harm, social disproval, or task failure; the feeling of empathy toward those who are in need or at risk; the feeling of responsibility that follows the recognition that one has caused distress or harm to another; the feeling of fatigue and/or ennui following repeated gratifications of a desire; and the feeling of uncertainty accompanying encounters with discrepant events that are not easily understood, or the detection of inconsistency among one's beliefs or between one's beliefs and actions.[31]

These feeling states represent the emotional substratum for a universal morality. Actions that accomplish the goals set by these various feeling states will be labeled virtuous, though the particular acts will depend upon a particular locale and historical situation. Moreover, it is these universally felt feeling states that form the basis for a virtue ethic, for they express a common experience (feeling state) that is concretized in a particular cultural setting.

I would agree with Kagan that the typical person relies less on sophisticated rational arguments (which is the "only" way for most philosophers) and more on feeling states to decide on the rightness or wrongness of an action. When working with clients in therapy, I repeatedly find they express evaluative judgments of right and wrong regarding the violation of standards associated with these feeling states: guilt, hurt, uncertainty. Their moral lives always make reference to these feeling states as the source for their discomfort and disappointment in their own self-esteem, which is tied to their own actions. Though at times not able to provide a well-argued philosophical or theological argument for their subjective distress, they "know" that they have not lived up to their own standards based on the intensity of their feelings.

An example that relates to this phenomenon was brought home to me recently. I was conducting a class for college freshmen on various ways young adults make moral decisions. We got unto a discussion of conflicts that occur between students and their parents. Several of the students bemoaned the fact that their parents either did not understand or kept too strict reins on their freedom when they came home for Christmas break. It soon became the general consensus of the class that parents were not sympathetic to their feelings or ideas. At this point, an administrator who sat in on the class spoke up. He reflected with the students on his role of being a father of two children. He spoke quite eloquently about how being a father was central to who he was as a person. He said, "You just want to love them and be everything you can for them and sometimes it just doesn't come out the way you want." Being a parent, in other words, spoke to very core of who he was as a person. It was fundamental to his own sense of being moral. I would suspect that nothing could hurt this man more than someone saying something like "you're not a good parent." It would wound him at his very core. As he spoke one could easily perceive the significance of family in this man's life. His personal investment in his children and the affective bond were intense and deep. His attachment to his children was, indeed, communicating knowledge. It was expressing his fundamental values. Above all this man wanted to be known as one who loves his family. More than anything, this role as parent reflected his sense of moral identity.

Other researchers point to specific feeling states such as shame and guilt as the "early moral emotions."[32] In essence these emotions serve as informative sources. That is, they bring to consciousness personal violations. In regards to a morality of the heart, early emotions such as shame and guilt "inform" the heart. Such feelings are best expressed as *affective knowledge* that orients the heart to care and sensitivity.

The *core* feeling of emotion (in comparison to cognition) can be easily demonstrated. Psychological studies of trauma victims show an often occurring phenomenon known as "survivor guilt." A common question such people ask is: "Why did I live while others died?" This feeling can be extraordinarily painful, particularly when those who have died are loved ones and/or one's relationship involved some measure of personal responsibility (e.g., parent, teacher). Though one might not be in any way at fault or could have done nothing to prevent the tragedy, many trauma victims do experience acute psychic pain and guilt. Even when one rationally goes over the accident and explains the situation and it turns out that the accident was unforeseen and absolutely nothing could have been done to prevent the tragedy, many people still experience guilt over the loss of others. In other words, reason does not eradicate the feeling. In fact, for such people emotion is a more central experience of their core sense of self. Fortunately, therapeutic approaches have been developed to treat such victims; nonetheless, the experience of negative feeling states points to the power of emotion as the core experience of moral selfhood.

A simple exercise might engage the reader. Go back to an experience in your life when something was explained to you that left you unconvinced. In other words, a situation existed where someone reasoned with you, presented a variety of facts, and articulated arguments that were coherent and sound. Nonetheless, upon hearing the explanation, you remark, "I understand what you're saying, but I still feel...." All of us have had such experiences. If you examine such an experience closely, it often results that it is one's feeling that represents what is a deeper truth. It is one's felt experience that is experienced more deeply.[33] This very simple exercise points, I think, to the fundamental centrality of the emotions in our daily (and moral) lives.

In sum, psychological studies suggest a significant role for emotion in the development of the moral life. Moreover, we have used a metaphor from botany and envisioned empathy as the foundational soil for a morality of the heart. If this is indeed the case, then emotions serve as the nutrients that nourish one's growing moral sensitivity and sustain moral growth and expanding moral vision.

From a perspective of care, the enduring power of emotion is best exemplified in the example of the administrator described above who spoke with intensity regarding his love for his family. Love's overwhelming importance for a heart morality accords it special consideration. In *The Broken Connection*, a provocative study of life and death imagery, psychiatrist Robert Jay Lifton describes the profound linkage of empathic experience as expressed through one's image-producing capacity with the emotion of love. He notes that "the emotion of loving" must be experienced as "a quality of perceiving the other's image-feelings so intensely as to approach sharing."[34] Though not naming the experience as an empathic one, Lifton's description of such image-experience is decidedly empathic in nature:

> The quality of that access to another's experience, physical and mental, is also specifically human. It is what makes possible the intense level of caring that can develop with love. That is why human beings can express and experience love in letters, on long-distance telephone, during and after prolonged physical separations, while being mostly indifferent to others immediately around them. So fundamental is this transformation that, in its absence, attachment or proximity becomes the enemy of vitality, and is deadening.[35]

Lifton notes that the word "emotion" is derived from the Latin *emovere*, which means "to move out, stir up, excite."[36] Emotion refers to movement toward or against. Moreover, emotion conveys the idea of relationship, some level of bonding to someone or something. Emotion signifies the appreciation and significance that an individual attaches to some person, object, or event within his or her environment.[37] To understand emotion, one must understand the relationships, motivations, and goals, as well as the significance (meanings) one attaches to the environment. Further, emotion serves as a source of *felt-intensity*. This intensity serves as a *value-evoking* experience. Emotional arousal, no matter what the attachment, whether it be to person or thing, renders in an explicit manner the *concerns of one's heart*. In this sense they are judgments that portray personal meaning: what is vital and, in the distinctive case of love, what is irrevocable for one's very meaning-existence. Quoting Robert Solomon, Lifton notes:

Emotions are self-involved and relatively *intense* evaluative judgments. They are always, whether implicitly or explicitly, judgments involving oneself as well as whatever else — disputes, cantaloupes, movies, other people or situations. The judgments and objects that constitute our emotions are those that are especially important to us, meaningful to us, concerning matters in which we have invested our Selves. Not surprisingly, most of our emotions involve other people, not only as their objects but also intersubjectively, in our concerns for our relationships, trust and intimacy, suspicion and betrayal, what others think of us as well as, insofar as we identify with them, what we think of them.[38]

Regarding the emotion of love, its experience is a meaningful investment of such intensity that the very disruption of love proves dangerously threatening.[39] Moreover, roles that express for us the centrality of love, become absolutely central for the defining and assessing of our selves as moral. Further, because these roles are so vital for our moral definition, their questioning renders us fragile and vulnerable. Recall the school administrator spoken of above. An accusation against this man questioning his ability to parent would create enormous psychological pain (and anger). I recall a painful encounter I once had with a close friend. This person had hurt me deeply. I confronted him on his behavior and I will never forget the look in his eyes when I brought the matter up with him. He found my confronting him an extraordinarily painful experience. As I reflect on those difficult moments together, I have come to see that his reaction made sense. My friend valued our friendship so highly that to question his behavior could not help but make him feel a moral vulnerability, for part of his felt experience of being moral was tied to the behavior he showed me as my friend. The words "parent," "friend," "spouse," "Good Samaritan," "person of integrity" or devotion to a cause or moral principle capture the essence of our moral definition, for they are the public proclamations of ourselves as moral persons. These roles represent that which is most dear. Think for a moment what you would experience if someone questioned your behavior as a spouse, friend, minister, or criticized the efforts that you have invested regarding some ministerial work or cause or principle that you deeply believe in.

To further elaborate, emotions reflect what psychologist Nico Frijda labels "the law of concern." In other words, emotions are the language that reflects that which is meaningful. "Emotions form the prime material in the exploration of an individual's concern."[40] We experience pain at the sight of a loved one's suffering and are angry when hurt by one that we love. In both instances, it is one's concern for the other (the value with which we hold the relationship and our personal investment within the relationship) that elicits the intensity of our emotions. In sum, love's significance emerges because it portrays that which is most meaningful as well as that to which we are most attached — the very core of *who we are*, part of which is our moral definition.

Thus far we have elaborated on the role of empathy and emotion in a heart morality. We have argued that empathic experience and emotion provide a fundamental understanding of morality that the impartiality of the justice principle is unable to address. Yet, such a morality also has its shortcomings.

The Psychologic of Billy Budd

A morality of the heart's dynamics might best be captured by turning to truth as so often expressed through literature. I would like to reflect on both the power and limitations of a heart morality through exploring Herman Melville's short story, *Billy Budd*.

The story was published in 1924, many years after Melville's death. Recently, this novella has become an instrument for dissecting values and for examining the moral actions of legal officials. As the *New York Times* noted when reporting on a law conference specifically designed to discuss Melville's story, "it is a story of innocence and evil, of crime and punishment, of rationality and insanity, of motives tainted and pure."[41]

The tale takes place against the background of the Napoleonic Wars. Already two mutinies have taken place in the royal navy, raising the fear of a fleet without discipline. Billy Budd is an impressed sailor known by everyone for his pleasant demeanor and innocent nature. A petty officer, Claggart, whose jealousy of Budd's innocence and goodness is absolute, falsely accuses Billy of mutiny before the ship's captain (Vere). Billy, who suffers from a speech impediment, is stunned by the accusation. In a brief moment of frenzied irrationality he strikes Claggart, wounding him mortally. The captain, portrayed as a just man, does not believe Claggart's accusation. Faced with the death of his petty officer and the charge of treason, he struggles with Billy's fate. In the end, a court martial is convened that leans toward a lesser judgment. The intercession of the captain, however, who feels himself duty-bound by the demands of martial law, leads to his condemnation and Billy is hanged.

The story has been portrayed as an allegory and moral fable. But what I would like to focus on is the relationship between the principal characters and what we might term the "psychologic" of the tale. "Billy, the handsome, strong, lovable sailor, represents the good tendencies, the tendencies often designated as 'the heart.'"[42] Billy's innocent character is contrasted to that of Claggart, who is the personification of evil. The petty officer is a bright man who recognizes the noble nature of Billy's character. It is Budd's goodness that triggers in Claggart an all-consuming hatred of who Billy is and what he represents.

When Captain Vere hears Claggart's accusations against Budd, he refuses to believe such charges:

> Though something exceptional in the moral quality of Captain Vere made him, in earnest encounter with a fellow man, a veritable touchstone of that man's essential nature, yet now as to Claggart and what was really going on in him his feelings partook less of intuitional convictions than of strong suspicion clogged by strange dubieties.[43]

The captain decides that the best way to resolve this unsettling question of Budd's guilt or innocence is to allow the two men to confront one another. Unfortunately, the unsuspecting sailor is initially rendered helpless by Claggart's indictment of his character:

Not at first did Billy take it in. When he did, the rose-tan of his cheek looked struck as by white leprosy. He stood like one impaled and gagged. Meanwhile the accuser's eyes, removing not as yet from the blue dilated ones, underwent a phenomenal change, their wonted rich violet color blurring into a muddly purple. Those lights of human intelligence, losing human expression, were gelidly protruding like the alien eyes of certain uncatalogued creatures of the deep. The first mesmeristic glance was one of serpent fascination; the last was as the paralyzing lurch of the torpedo fish.[44]

Vere, unaware of Billy's speech impediment, implores the young sailor to defend himself. " 'Speak, man!' said Captain Vere to the transfixed one, struck by his aspect even more than by Claggart's. 'Speak. Defend yourself!' "[45] Billy's speechlessness is apparent and the captain intuits rightly Billy's problem, having remembered a similar incident with a classmate during his school days. The captain changes his approach and gently cajoles Budd to respond. "Going close up to the young sailor, and laying a soothing hand on his shoulder, he said, 'There is no hurry, my boy. Take your time, take your time.' "[46] Unfortunately, this altered approach reflecting words of care not only fails to have the desired effect but provides the trigger for tragic consequences.

Melville captures poignantly the reaction in Billy and the effects stemming from Claggart's deceit:

Contrary to the effect intended, these words so fatherly in tone, doubtless touching Billy's heart to the quick, prompted yet more violent efforts at utterance — efforts soon ending for the time in confirming the paralysis, and bringing up to his face an expression that was a crucifixion to behold. The next instant, quick as the flame from a discharged cannon at night, his right hand shot out, and Claggart dropped to the deck.[47]

It is interesting to note that the captain's soothing words upset even more the young sailor's heart, prompting an instantaneous yet violent response. One critic notes that a line that was not used in the final version of the story describes Billy's striking of Claggart as "electrically energized by the inmost spasm of his heart."[48] In essence, it is in the recesses of Billy's heart that he lashes out at the evil he encounters from Claggart's duplicity.

Upon the death of Claggart, the story moves swiftly to examining the fate of Billy. Though this moral tale is fraught with legal questions (e.g., Should Billy be brought to trial? If so, should the trial be held now or later — when the ship arrives back in port? Should he be found innocent or guilty?), an equally significant question is the *quality* of Billy and Vere's relationship and its influence on their unfolding futures.

The ensuing events highlight what bonds them together. Vere believes legal recourse must occur immediately lest knowledge of the incident awaken disloyal attitudes among the crew. He convenes a summary court and serves as the only witness, detailing the tragic events. The three-man officer court is shocked at hearing the recounting of the confrontation between the two antagonists and subsequent events. When responding to the captain's account, Billy acknowledges the events as the captain describes them but denies vehemently the truth of Claggart's words. The captain shows that even he believes that Billy is innocent of mutiny when he says, "I believe you my man."[49] Billy expresses remorse at Claggart's death, but explains that "he foully lied to my face and in presence of my captain, and I had to say something, and I could only say it with a blow, God help me!"[50] With the dismissal of Billy, the court and Vere are left to determine his fate. All present are troubled by the incident. But Vere eloquently charges them to their duties as officers. Through Vere, Melville again taps the meaning of heart. "But the exceptional in the matter moves the hearts within you. Even so too is mine moved. But let not warm hearts betray heads that should be cool."[51] Under martial law, extenuating circumstances are irrelevant; consequently, capital punishment is the only recourse.

As the captain speaks he indirectly makes reference to the empathic expression that so typifies the demeanor of Budd. "'But did he know our hearts, I take him to be of that generous nature that he would feel even for us on whom in this military necessity so heavy a compulsion is laid."[52] As if fate would have it no other way, Billy is convicted and sentenced to hang.

What follows is a rich description of humanity that is tragic, yet gracious in its nobility. Vere himself communicates to Billy the sentence of the court. Melville describes how this private communication remains forever a private matter between the captain and his sailor. Yet the narrator speculates as to what occurred between them. For one, Vere probably was honest with Billy about his own role and troubled thoughts that led him to sway the court to hand down its final verdict. "On Billy's side it is not improbable that such a confession would have been received in much the same spirit that prompted it."[53] Even more poignantly, the narrator speculates as to the depth of Vere's own feelings:

> He was old enough to have been Billy's father. The austere devotee of military duty, letting himself melt back into what remains primeval in our formalized humanity, may in end have caught Billy to his heart, even as Abraham may have caught young Isaac on the brink of resolutely offering him up in obedience to the exacting behest.[54]

Upon completion of the conversation, Vere is first encountered by the lieutenant, whose reaction is described as follows:

> The face he beheld, for the moment one expressive of the agony of the strong, was to that officer, though a man of fifty, a startling revelation. That the condemned one suffered less than he who mainly had effected the condemnation was apparently indicated by the former's exclamation in the scene soon perforce to be touched upon.[55]

In the end, Billy's fate is sealed. Yet, immediately prior to his hanging he nobly utters his famous words. "At the penultimate moment, his words, his only ones, words wholly unobstructed in the utterance, were these: 'God bless Captain Vere!'" The narrator continues:

> Without volition, as it were, as if indeed the ship's populace were but the vehicles of some current electric, with one voice from alow and aloft came a resonant sympathetic echo: "God bless Captain Vere!" And yet at that instant Billy alone must have been in their hearts, even as in their eyes.[56]

What are we to make of such a story? This work can be read on many levels. Scholar Grant Watson witnesses to its enduring truth when he notes:

> In this short history of the impressment and hanging of a handsome sailor-boy, are to be discovered problems almost as profound as those that puzzle us in the pages of the Gospels. *Billy Budd* is a book to be read many times, for at each reading it will

light up, as do the greater experiences of life, a beyond leading always into the unknown.[57]

The story of *Billy Budd* raises stark questions about law: its adequacy and imperfection. In addition, though, the relationship of Vere and Budd, two souls drawn together in a tragic way, serve as instruments through their own relationship to broaden the moral domain regarding the meaning of sensitivity, the struggle for moral integrity in the midst of the complex, and the quest for a moral vision.

I wish to focus attention on the dynamics of the relationship between Budd and Vere. More specifically, I wish to comment on the role of empathy. The attraction of Vere or Budd to the reader to a significant degree rests on this empathic sense. As one follows Vere as he communicates to Billy the judgment of the court, one can be led to be a helpless yet pained observer as the two souls privately communicate the intentions and feelings at this tragic turn of events. Within their conversation, one is led to image the struggle of each as they face Billy's fate. Indeed, Vere emerges shaken from such an encounter and Billy is viewed as having "suffered less." It is their empathy for one another that insures their moral character in the eyes of the reader. In some unfathomable way, they are now tied to one another — bonded in a quest for moral truth.

For Vere, this empathic bonding challenges him to a greater realization of law's limits and the accompanying self-knowledge such revelation entails. More than ever before, he has come, through his empathy for Billy, to realize the law's inadequacy as well as a greater understanding of his own self (best portrayed through his feelings of fatherhood for Billy). One might reasonably conclude that in the future Vere would become a changed man, or at least one who has been allowed a new way of seeing, leading to an expanded moral vision. More than likely, future questions of law and compassion will evoke from him a greater appreciation of the complexities and an even greater awareness of his own self as a sensitive and feeling soul. For the young sailor there emerges an inner integrity and commitment to moral purpose. The words "God bless Captain Vere," upon reflection, are what the reader would expect from someone like Billy as the innocence and goodness of his character is portrayed throughout the story. Moreover, I would conclude that it was his empathy for Vere, more than anything else, that allowed him to utter these words. No doubt in their private conversation, forever kept from the reader, Billy could empathize with Vere's struggle.

The story of Billy Budd portrays the complexity of morality as well as the limits of a heart morality. What type of morality could without qualification tell us what is the "moral" thing to do? The reader is haunted by a plethora of moral questions: What can we say about Billy's acceptance of his fate? Can compassion rightfully overcome the demands of law? Was justice served in this situation? Are law and morality the same? Must our hearts always be compromised by the realities of the complex? Is there ever "one" moral response that emerges more compelling than all others? One is also confronted with the moral ambiguity of emotions. No doubt Claggart's charges enraged Billy. His feelings of anger at being so falsely accused did violence to his self. Combined with his inability to express himself, his rage surfaced through physical violence. Was this act one of insanity? If not, was it justified? Does it not show that emotion can be blind?

No doubt reason and the heart are continually challenging us in this story. Yet empathy does serve a vital function that in the end strengthens the heart's resolve. Empathy serves to endear the story to the reader as each of us attempts to understand the struggle of Vere and the fate of Billy, thereby insuring the enduring nature of the moral questions raised. Likewise, empathy is integral to understanding the relationship of Vere and Billy. And it is this very empathic expression that serves to sensitize one man to the possibility of future moral sensitivity (Vere) and the other to commitment to his own integrity (Budd).

Though empathic expression, particularly as manifested through a heart morality, cannot resolve the numerous moral issues at hand in this story, they do further moral growth. The point to be made with the empathy dynamic present in *Billy Budd* is the vital role that empathic experiences have in allowing us either to live out our own sense of moral integrity (in the case of Billy) or the role they serve in helping to awaken within us ambiguity and the complexity of moral situations, thereby preparing us to be more present to the complexity and perspectives of future moral encounters (hopefully the case for Vere). In sum, though empathic experience might not resolve complex moral questions, it serves to engender deepening sensitivity as well as to expand our moral horizon. In sum, as one critic describes this story's effects:

> United now, the beautiful and the good create a vision larger than either, a vision transcending the case of Billy Budd or the quandary of Captain Vere. The teller, now any man, presents man's feelings in the face of any great dilemma. Thought and feeling, outdistancing themselves, become objects of contempla-

tion, remote yet immediate. The effect of this form is moral in the sense of enlarging our awareness of human conditions or relationships and of improving our sensitivity.[58]

The Heart's Other Side

Though the overwhelming impression one has of the "heart" is apt to be that of caring sensitivity and love, it is not necessarily so. Indeed, the heart's power can be hardened and limited, even devoid of its own loving presence. According to Rahner, the word "heart"

> does not denote simply and immediately love. This inward-corporeal core of the personal being of man, which borders on the source of all mystery, can according to Scripture also be evil and the bottomless pit, into which the evil-doer who shuts himself off from love plunges. The heart can be empty of love, and even what can still be called love can be very peripheral.[59]

One is reminded of Conrad's short story the *Heart of Darkness*, where the depravity of the character Kurtz is complete. Theologian Steven Duffy has reflected on "our hearts of darkness" by examining the question of evil in light of twentieth-century thought and culture.[60] In sum, the recesses of the heart are never totally appropriated in loving self-sacrifice, for every heart is compromised by the finitude and egotism so pervasive within the human condition.

From the standpoint of our psychological exploration, however, the point I wish to stress is the capacity of emotion to warp the heart's commitment to loving sacrifice. The destruction of the heart's potential for good might arise from psychological factors. The tragic nature of child abuse and domestic violence can, for example, foster in children such deep-seated emotional reactions — like the inability to trust, character disorders, and crippled emotional lives — that one's heart is forever compromised. Just as emotion helps to focus a sense of care, it is also a force for holding the heart hostage. In a world filled with stress, misunderstandings, and everyday complexities that all too often seem to inundate our lives, it becomes quite easy for us to imprison ourselves with frustration, negative attitudes, and hurt feelings. At times these feelings can be extraordinarily painful, and they often absorb our psychic energies while blinding our moral vision. There often transpires an immense struggle in "letting go" of these feelings.

Such feelings are apt to be particularly strong when they involve questions of personal integrity or what we view as a normal rights and expectations (the right at least to have our voice heard and taken into consideration):

Because people's moral motivations are strong, they become emotional when possibilities arise that they will be found out not to be moral, or that they will be victimized ("screwed," to use the students' word), or be excluded from a dialogue that involves their self-interest. The words for the reactions that follow the obstruction of moral motivations are all emotion words: outrage, indignation, disgrace, shame, umbrage, taken-in, cheated, belittled, ripped-off, and so forth. And they follow not just the obstruction of moral motivation; even the threat of obstruction is sufficient.[61]

The reader might reflect, for example, on a situation in his or her own life when injustice occurred: he felt cheated or she was not given a chance to defend herself. What emerges from such conflict is an enormous level of moral indignation that in turn engenders outrage, anger, and distrust. In the immediacy of the situation emotions are oftentimes blind and all-consuming. Even with restitution or a change in events, our emotions are apt to remain negative and linger on.

Usually, when we are able to develop a proper perspective and get the necessary distance from our previous negativity, we wonder why we became so preoccupied with the hurt feeling or how we allowed ourselves to become so blind or were unable to give up such feelings. There is a simple answer to such a question — it is *human*. By "human" I mean that in some sense our lives are endowed to keep the experience of painful emotion conscious. To elaborate, each of us experiences a certain amount of joy and love in our lives that is nurturing and sustaining for life functioning. Yet if inquiry were made as to the most emotionally intense experiences of our lives, in all likelihood a majority of them would be tinged with negative and painful feelings. In short, positive experiences drift slowly away and we almost effortlessly become preoccupied with the wounded feelings surrounding negative reactions and personal disappointments. In a sense, as humans we are oriented to dwell on the negative.

Why is this so? The answer resides in the role of emotions in our lives. Recall that emotions can loosely be defined as subjective experiences of various intensity that dispose us to some type of action-ready state. They proclaim our valued concerns and orient us to a distinct behavioral path. This dwelling on negative emotions can best be described through "the Law of Hedonic Asymmetry."[62] Briefly, joy and satisfaction are apt to fade from memory and consciousness whereas hurt and pain are apt to linger, remaining intrusively conscious. "The law predicts a negative balance for the quality of life, unless self-deceit and self-defense intervene, which of course they do."[63] The joys of life are all too often memories that are fleeting whereas the pains and hurts remain more conscious. You might be complimented or helped by a close, trusted friend, yet if this same friend betrays your confidence over an important matter or hurts you deeply, which experience are you apt to remember a year from now? We rejoice over the memory of the good times with a deceased family member or good friend, yet can the intensity of that joy match the shock at receiving the phone call announcing the loved one's death or the visual memory of watching him or her slowly die? A vacation brings us a well-deserved rest, yet how sustaining is this feeling when one encounters the pressures and stress of everyday work or the optimistic promises we made to limit our work? "The law of hedonic asymmetry is a stern and bitter law."[64] Its purpose is vital, however, for human functioning. Recall that emotions are subjective states that ready us for action. From an evolutionary perspective, for survival one must realize, understand, and be prepared to react to the struggles and painful experiences of life. This "shows the human mind to have been made not for happiness, but for instantiating the blind biological laws of survival."[65] Emotions serve as a vital link in this survival process by preparing us for action.

Though we are all held captive at times by negative emotions, they need not imprison us. We can actively counter this predisposition through *effort*. We can channel our energies into recalling positive experiences, moments of satisfaction and joy, and instances of serenity and peace.

On the other hand, the law's outcomes are not unavoidable. Adaptation to satisfaction can be counteracted by constantly being aware of how fortunate one's condition is and of how it could have been otherwise, or actually was otherwise before — by rekindling impact through recollection and imagination. Enduring happiness seems possible, and it can be understood theoretically. However, note that it does not come naturally, by itself. It takes effort.[66]

What might instill effortful actions that break the shackles of hurt feelings, bitterness, and ill will that so often imprison us? One experience in particular is apt to offer hope for freeing our hearts. This experience is gratitude. We will examine gratitude at greater length in chapter 6 when we offer some pastoral suggestions for guiding ministerial practice.

Conscience: The Human Mechanism for Living a "Morality of the Heart"

In our discussion thus far we have chosen "heart" as the basic metaphor for understanding an empathically-based morality. In this regard, emotion serves as a nutrient for furthering our moral vision for it serves as a form of affective knowledge that points out our fundamental concerns and desires. Once again, the thinking of psychologist Norma Haan proves helpful:

> Emotions accompany and enrich understandings, and they convey far more authentic information about a person's position in a dispute than any well-articulated thoughts. In ordinary circumstances, emotions instruct and energize action. In situations of great moral costs, emotions can overwhelm and disorganize cognitive activity.[67]

At the same time, we have also seen the power of emotions to blind and distort the heart.

As we have discussed, the moral psychology of Kohlberg falls short in understanding key factors in moral development: moral sensitivity, character, and moral vision. At the same time, a heart morality must encompass some parameters lest it become unwieldy. In other words, in everyday human experience, we must be able to conceptualize an empathically-based morality's linkage with moral growth. I believe the optimum approach for this linkage surfaces when we incorporate empathy and emotion within everyday human decision making as expressed through the functioning of conscience.

I have explored elsewhere a seven-dimensional model for conscience that forms the basis for a conscience of other-centered value.[68] In popular terms, conscience is most often equated with "right and wrong" or rules and their violation. Though to an extent there is truth to this perspective, such narrow viewing of conscience limits its meaning and deprives it of richness and complexity. Equally important, such a circumscribed definition of conscience fails to account for the working of conscience in everyday life.

By framing conscience in the context of "other-centered value," we are attempting to address the need to respond to the Lord's call to act lovingly in everyday life situations. A conscience of "other-centered value" provides for communal bonding and relational commitment. It recognizes the need for loving self-sacrifice and the taking of personal responsibility for one's actions. In sum, our view of conscience addresses the need to incorporate cognitive, affective, and intrapsychic processes, all of which are indispensable for moral functioning. And since moral growth can only take place in the midst of everyday human functioning, we must address how our humanity provides for moral growth. By exploring the psychology of conscience of "other-centered value" we link human experience with moral growth.

Below we explore briefly each of conscience's seven dimensions. In order to give clarity to our understanding, we then analyze one of the characters in the film *Rain Man* and show how the moral growth of Charlie Babbitt can best be explained by a conscience of other-centered value, and particularly its dimension of empathy.

Adaptive Psychic Energy. Psychic energy represents the psychological fuel for adaptive, healthy functioning. Our emotions, dreams, fantasy, and thought are all products of the psyche's expenditure of energy. We can best view this energy by exploring our attachments and on what we focus. In other words, in what do we invest our lives? What takes up our time? Psychic energy has two features. The way we focus and attend goes a long way in determining future growth and life accomplishments. For example, an adolescent who spends excessive time in front of a TV or engages in self-injurious behavior (drug taking) will inevitably close off or limit options for him or herself.

The second feature of psychic energy is its finite nature. If we attend and focus on some people, objects, or goals, then, by necessity, other people, objects, and goals are left unattended. Psychic energy is best utilized when channeled into completing appropriate developmental tasks and working through in a constructive way developmental and everyday life conflicts. Proper use of our psychic energies allows for self-reflection and adequate emotional functioning that is essential for authentic moral decision making.

Healthy Defensive Functioning. As we noted above, defense mechanisms are psychological processes we employ to lessen anxiety and bolster self-esteem. We have already noted the immature defense mechanisms that limit moral growth. On the other hand, there exist a group of defense mechanisms that, when properly employed, foster moral growth and maturing behaviors, that allow for successful coping with stress and successful negotiation of ambiguous, complex, and threatening life events. These include sublimation, sense of humor, role flexibility, suppression (the capacity to inhibit impulses), identification (having mature and healthy role models), realistic anticipation, and altruism.

Guilt. Guilt is integral for healthy conscience functioning. To be sure, unhealthy aspects of guilt are crippling. They include weakened self-esteem, depression, a sense of personal devaluation, and compensating behaviors that often take on a compulsive quality. Still, guilt is vital for moral growth. Admittedly the experience of guilt is one of the most difficult psychological tightropes to walk. That is, if experienced too intensely its effects can be damaging. On the other hand, to deny the experience of guilt deprives one of a naturally occurring psychic experience whose function nourishes sensitivity and altruistic response.

Idealization. A crucially important aspect of conscience is the idealizing qualities that tap our dreams, hopes, and deepest desires. In other words, conscience includes not only the discernment of "right and wrong" but what might be termed metaquestions — those inquiries that frame our lives and hopes: What do I dream for? What are my deepest desires? What am I becoming? What are the images that guide my life?

Empathy. Empathy provides the capacity needed for responding to another and the human sensitivity required for bonding. Moreover, without empathy one would be hard pressed to realize the effects of one's own actions on others. Further, empathy provides the capacity for shared experience, a process critical for moral growth.

Self-esteem. Self-esteem reflects a felt sense of inner goodness. Without this experience, one is often overly inhibited or unable to take the necessary steps to further moral growth. Further, it is self-esteem that allows one to come to self-honesty. Having adequate self-esteem provides sturdy psychological support for necessary self-scrutiny, which includes examining the darkness and unexplored areas of one's life.

Teleology. Underlying moral growth is the "sake for which" we do something. The telic dimension of conscience challenges us to think why we do what we do. It points to the personal responsibility we must take for our actions and the responsible use of our freedom. Each person must examine the fundamental orientation to value that guides his or her own life. It is through this process of self-examination that we take personal responsibility for our actions and ultimately the lifelong project of fashioning our moral vision.

To summarize, our hypothesis is that our everyday decisions that incorporate the Gospel command to love are best understood by attending to human experience that includes cognitive, affective, and intrapsychic features. The seven-dimensional view of conscience we propose attends to these features and provides the human mechanism for carrying out the heart morality we have proposed. By examining the movie *Rain Man*, we can appreciate how a heart morality and a conscience of "other-centered value" are linked as well as see the significance they exercise in developing moral sensitivity, character, and moral vision.[69]

At the beginning of the film we are introduced to a young adult named Charlie Babbitt (played by actor Tom Cruise), a slick, conniving businessman who is "nothing more than a used-car salesman operating on a borrowed shoestring."[70] Charlie is the classic fast-buck artist who is always looking for the quick sale. Whether in business dealings or personal relationships, Charlie seeks to exploit the vulnerability in the other, the opening that gives him advantage and control.

The audience discovers Charlie's dire financial straits and his shady business dealings. Soon Charlie has something else to preoccupy himself. While driving away with his girlfriend for a weekend, Charlie gets a call on his car phone informing him of his father's death. As is typical, Charlie displays no emotion on learning the news, and after flying to Cincinnati (his boyhood home) for the funeral he and his girl friend stop over at his deceased father's house. The house brings up memories and Charlie reminisces about his hatred for his father and how he left home in his teenage years. He recalls his painful attempts to please his father that always came up short. His grades, even when good, were never good enough. His sports' accomplishments could have always been better. In short, nothing pleased him.

That was it, the whole story. The story of a boy who

ran away from an implacable, domineering father for whom the son was never good enough, a boy who was spending his valuable life trying to prove to that father that he *was* good enough, only now it was too late. His father would never recognize his successes now, nor any more judge his failures. His father would never be proud of him.[71]

Charlie reveals to Susanna that to assuage his loneliness and pained feelings he took refuge in fantasy by listening to a "pretend friend" ("Rain Man") who sang to him.

Unfortunately for Charlie, his meeting with his father's lawyer to go over the will becomes another disappointment. He is jolted to learn that he has been eliminated from his father's three-million-dollar estate. His anger turns to rage over being "shut out" of what he perceives as rightfully his. His frustration only increases when he learns that he has an institutionalized older brother, Raymond (played by actor Dustin Hoffman), and that the estate has been left with a trustee to provide for his brother's care.

Angered by what he considers an injustice, Charlie kidnaps Raymond in hopes of negotiating his brother's return for half the estate. What follows is a marathon odyssey. The two drive from Cincinnati to Charlie's home in Los Angeles. The attention of the viewer is often riveted on Raymond's incredible powers; he is an autistic savant — a person usually of limited intelligence who nonetheless possesses extraordinary powers of genius for numerical computation or other equally amazing feats. Nonetheless, the "heart" of the film revolves around Charlie's growing moral sensitivity. Indeed, the exchanges between Charlie and Raymond on their journey to California enable us to see a moral transformation in the younger brother. The funny, angry, and at times exasperating exchanges between these two misfit brothers gradually lead Charlie to pry loose his veneer of self-absorption and slowly experience the true meaning of sensitivity, compassion, and love.

It is an analysis of Charlie's conscience as outlined above that allows us to understand how this moral growth has taken place.

First, Charlie's psychic energies have been dissipated on non-growthful activities and using others. He has never worked through his own developmental needs (e.g., identity, intimacy) or conflicts (his relationship with his father). In having to care for his brother (buying him food, providing for his needs) Charlie begins to focus on his needs for attachment and investment in a caring and nurturing relationship.

When Charlie leaves Cincinnati with Raymond, his defenses are well in place. He rationalizes that he is entitled to half the estate and that kidnapping Raymond is a solution to his financial problems. He minimizes using Raymond for his own ends. He shows no hesitation in blaming his father for their estrangement (externalizing). Ineluctably, however, these defenses are whittled away as the fumbling, endearing, and at times tragic character of Raymond lures Charlie to express brotherly protection and care.

It would be hard to imagine the Charlie we first encounter in the film to be a man with guilt. Toward the end, though, Charlie is Raymond's advocate, pleading with officials to allow Raymond to remain with him in California even though there is no longer any possibility of gaining any financial reward. Charlie's growing attachment to Raymond triggers self-examination of his previous intentions, thereby fostering some level of guilt.

The film gives only brief glimpses into what ideals and dreams are meaningful in Charlie's life. Yet by the end of the film, if you asked Charlie what the word "brother" signifies in his life, his answer, spoken from his heart, would reflect a deepening level of commitment and fidelity. Through his growing love for his brother, Charlie realizes his own needs for affection and family. Although he was never before committed to anyone or anything, the word "brother" now represents for him the ideal that guides his life, thereby providing some evaluative dimension for his actions. As Raymond's brother, Charlie comes to learn the meaning of loyalty, mutuality, and forgiveness. He experiences for the first time the meaning of "family" and discovers his own need for others.

More than any other dimension, empathy proves a catalyst for Charlie's growth. As he experiences his brother he is drawn to reflect on his own childhood and is able to construct his previous life as a wounded child, a life he is now able to admit to and explore through his experiences with Raymond. In a powerful motel room scene he makes a connection with his childhood and realizes that the "Rain Man" he fondly found refuge in was actually "Raymond," his newly discovered brother. Charlie realizes through Raymond's reaction to running water and his pained utterances that Raymond was sent away because he accidently scalded Charlie when he attempted to imitate their deceased mother and bathe him just as their mother had done. Ironically, the well intentioned but helpless older brother was banished for simply trying *to be* his brother, for actually trying to provide Charlie the care he always needed. "Charlie fell silent, still wrapped in astonishment. He looked at his brother, his autistic brother who'd been locked away for twenty-four years, his brother whom once he'd loved and needed with a baby's dependence and then forgotten and transformed into something imaginary."[72] Such emotional bonding more than cements their lives together. It forces Charlie to view himself not as isolated and self-absorbed but as one connected and related. His life will never again be the same. Later in the film the audience is treated to the endearing, comical scene of Charlie showing Raymond how to dance. Watching them as dance partners, one strongly resonates with Charlie's newly found brotherly love.

> A sudden wave of unexpected affection washed over Charlie, and for a moment he forgot himself. For the space of a handful of heartbeats Charlie forgot who and what Raymond was, remembering only that this was his brother. His brother Rain Man. Grabbing Raymond tightly, he hugged him hard.[73]

The lingering effects of Charlie's painful relationship with his father, of which we have only glimpses through his brief recollections, point to fragile self-esteem. Nothing Charlie ever did was right. Perhaps selling cars and living in the fast lane serve to fill the void he feels within. By the end of the film, however, Charlie seems revitalized. The viewer begins to perceive Charlie in a new light, as a person who has found some moral certainty and felt sense of inner goodness.

Finally, Charlie comes to embrace moral responsibility. He desires, after their journey, to establish custody of his brother and provide for him. At an evaluation hearing before the psychiatrist, Charlie articulates a reasoned moral stance. He has come to value Raymond for who he is and not for what he might use him for. In addition, he genuinely wishes what is good for Raymond, even though it might mean separation and Raymond's return to Cincinnati. In the end, unfortunately, it becomes obvious that Raymond is in need of institutional care and must depart and return to Cincinnati. Charlie is again alone, but his life has changed. Charlie can accept Raymond's leaving as in his older brother's best interest, yet at the same time remain committed to this newly found relationship. At the train station Charlie tells Raymond that he will see him again in a couple of weeks. This promise of a visit is evidence of Charlie's moral growth, the expression of moral commitment threaded with fidelity.

Charlie has hardly become a saint; indeed, there remains much room for growth. We could confidently conclude that Charlie will still appreciate the quick sale, at times use others, and display a chip on his shoulder wondering if life is ever fair. Yet he is *not* the same character we encountered at the film's beginning. Charlie has grown morally. His conscience has allowed him to glimpse what is nobly profound within human experience. Through peering within and relating to the self-absorbed world of Raymond's frailty, Charlie experiences an awakening of moral sensitivity, begins to comprehend the meaning of moral character, and expands his own moral vision that now has come to include the needs of others, thereby insuring that his future relationships and dealings are irrevocably altered.

This analysis of *Rain Man* points out the role of conscience in fostering the moral life. Kohlberg's moral psychology is unable to provide a coherent explanation for Charlie's growth. Only a heart morality can account for the Charlie at the film's ending who cares deeply for his brother. The various dimensions of conscience outlined above demonstrate how this self-absorbed character grows morally through deciding for other-centered value. Furthermore, the dimension of empathy takes on special significance. Empathy allows for his bonding to Raymond and provides the possibility for him to experience their shared lives together that in turn stimulates his self-scrutiny as to what is truly significant and meaningful for him.

> In many ways Charlie was exactly like Raymond. Raymond too had to fight to survive. Raymond too had built an elaborate set of defence mechanisms that walled him off from others. Deep down Charlie, just like Raymond, was afraid to be touched. Charlie and Raymond had each created a world that he alone inhabited; both Raymond and Charlie were the sole centers of their existence, interested in nothing except what affected their personal comfort or safety.
>
> The difference was that Raymond had been born deficient, while Charlie had attained his deficiency through hard work and constant practice. Raymond couldn't connect with another human being because he'd been damaged and a vital piece of his brain was missing, the piece that communicated. Charlie couldn't connect with anybody because he'd forced himself to forget how. Feelings slowed him down and got in his way. For the first time Charlie Babbitt realized what he'd been doing to himself all these years, how he'd cut himself off, insulated himself from uncomfortable human emotions. And he realized something else too, something even more important. Raymond had never been close to another human being because *he could not*; Charlie had never been close to another human being because *he would not*.[74]

Following Charlie's journey of moral growth makes it clear that it is his empathic experience that offers him the possibility to examine his life with honest self-scrutiny. It is his empathic experience shown through his shared history with Raymond and his feeling for him that engenders his growing insight into and evaluation of who he is, what he has become. Kohlberg's moral psychology cannot account for Charlie's moral development.

This chapter has explored the use of a heart morality to examine the significance of empathy and emotion for the moral life. We have viewed the power of empathy and emotion to foster moral growth as well as looked at their limitation. One final piece of our exploration remains to be uncovered. The heart morality and its accompanying emotions (e.g., love, guilt, anger arising from injustice) need an adequate vision; otherwise, such emotions can themselves be blind. To this task we now turn.

$\succ$ *Chapter 5* $\prec$

Christian Empathy:
The Heart's Vision

More tortuous than all else is the human heart, beyond remedy; who can understand it? I, the Lord, alone probe the mind and test the heart, to reward everyone according to his ways, according to the merit of his deeds.

—Jeremiah 17:9–10

Religious educator John Elias notes that "in the most recent criticisms of the public schools and colleges of this country politicians, educators, and ordinary citizens have called upon the schools to involve themselves in moral education or education in values."[1] This refocusing on values is one of the most encouraging stories in contemporary education. Gone are the days when value neutrality was the only acceptable perspective from which to teach. American society is once again aware of the vital role values occupy in educational life. Value neutrality has yielded to the realization that some values are, indeed, "good" or preferred over others. As we enter upon the last decade of the twentieth century, there is growing emphasis on the communitarian nature necessary for society's survival. A vital ingredient for such functioning is consensual agreement regarding a core set of values that sustain society's moral climate. Moreover, a "shift" has taken place in public attitudes and questions of a "public morality" occupy center stage.

During most of the twentieth century, first artists and intellectuals, then broader segments of the society, challenged every convention, every prohibition, every regulation that cramped the human spirit or blocked its appetites and ambitions. Today, a reaction has set in, born of a recognition that the public needs common standards to hold a diverse society together, to prevent ecological disaster, to maintain confidence in government, to conserve scarce resources, to escape disease, to avoid the inhumane applications of technology. This new respect for limits is bound to carry with it a concern for the moral values and restraints that unify communities and keep human conduct within acceptable bounds.[2]

And, as psychologist Thomas Lickona notes, "'There is a hunger for morality in the land. ... People really do want to create a society where they can count on their neighbors to be decent human beings. The schools can't ignore them and the families know they can't do it alone.'"[3]

A recent article in the *New York Times* documents this trend. School districts today are busy drawing up lists of core values. This willingness to consider the endorsement of some values as an essential component of student education finds a parallel movement in higher education circles. Each year colleges and universities offer a wide variety of courses on ethical issues ranging from moral reasoning analysis for freshman to professional ethics seminars across a wide variety of disciplines for graduate students. Moreover, this focus is not limited to students; administrators, faculty members, and staff are being pushed to consider the need to take moral responsibility and view the ethical dimension of their work. According to educator Rachelle Hollander, "Educational institutions are finding themselves in the position of being challenged to develop guidelines for their members along various fronts, all falling under the rubric of ethics."[4] And Harvard president Derek Bok remarks:

Nothing is so likely to produce cynicism, especially among those taking courses in practical ethics, as a realization that the very institution that offers such classes shows little concern for living up to its own moral obligations.[5]

Yet education is not alone in rethinking the need for values. Political theory, particularly contemporary liberal theory, is currently undergoing self-scrutiny.[6] Traditionally, liberal democratic theory has championed rights and individual liberties. But can such a hallowed role for liberty be taken too far? Is there not need for a consensus of values that underlies a moral foundation without which liberty becomes a license simply for the atomization of each of society's members? Currently, some political thinkers are reconsidering the need for a vision of the common good upon which citizens can agree. For too long, liberal theory has endorsed the role of the individual without considering the needs of the community and the vital role that cooperation and interdependence exercise in society's functioning.

Social scientists are also addressing this issue. Sociologist Amitai Etzioni has recently argued that social science has for too long been guided by the erroneous notion that people are guided by their self-interest. Within this perspective, individuals make rational decisions that maximize their own gain. The problem with this model of decision making, says Etzioni, is that people often make decisions on other than rational grounds. What is needed is a new model that explains how people do indeed make everyday decisions. Etzioni notes:

> The idea that most people's choices are influenced heavily by their values and emotions provides a beginning. Entire categories of means to ends, whether efficient or not, are judged to be unacceptable and are automatically ruled out. For example, about a third of the people entitled to welfare benefits refuse to apply on the ground that "it's not right." While emotions and values are often depicted as distorting rationality (which they do), they also influence people against using means that may be efficient in the narrow sense but are wrong or hurtful to others. That is, our values influence both our choice of goals and the way we proceed to accomplish them.[7]

Etzioni goes on to note a rational approach guided by self-interest dominates social science research, education, and public policy. This myopic view ignores the importance of community and moral and social values necessary for developing humane social policies.

A devastating critique of the rational approach and the self-interest model is provided by economist Robert Frank in his provocative study, *Passions within Reason*.[8] Frank challenges social science's bias toward individualism and personal aggrandizement. In opposition to the self-interest model championed by social scientists, Frank proposes the commitment model. In essence, this model maintains that behavior viewed as irrational is often best understood through emotional tendencies that sustain one's commitments. "On purely theoretical grounds, the commitment model suggests that the moving force behind moral behavior lies not in rational analysis but in the emotions."[9] Self-interest models cannot explain the presence of innumerable examples of "virtuous behaviors" that are so readily practiced by many people, particularly when such behaviors lead to self-sacrifice and personal hardship.

What leads people to behave in altruistic ways and defy their immediate self-interest? The experience of emotions becomes central:

> Consider, for example, a person capable of strong guilt feelings. This person will not cheat even when it is in her material interests to do so. The reason is not that she fears getting caught but that she simply does not *want* to cheat. Her aversion to feelings of guilt effectively alters the payoffs she faces.[10]

In essence, her emotions create "costs" and help to contain the lack of impulse control that plagues so many others. Rationalist interpretations that champion self-interest fail to take such feelings into account.

Similarly, a morality of the heart endorses care, sensitivity toward others, and basic core values such as honesty and self-sacrifice. Moreover, empathic and corresponding emotional expressions provide the human capacity for interrelationship. Such experiences (empathic arousal, guilt, love) stir one to endure hardship and self-sacrifice that often accompany altruistic action. Speaking at his inaugural as president of Brown University, educator Vartan Gregorian eloquently noted:

> We have no choice but to end the imprisonment of the self and concern ourselves with those outside our moral enclosures. We need a moral center, not a moral enclosure. We need to be capable of moral outrage and sensitive to the pain and sorrow of our fellow man and woman. It is important not only to be able to engage in new ideas, but also to be willing to make public declarations of one's convictions and commitments and then translate them into actions and deeds.[11]

The empathically based heart morality we have proposed makes viable this "moral center." The ideas expressed by Gregorian — sensitivity, the capacity for "moral outrage," and the translation of one's commitments into actions and deeds — are integrally tied to our capacity for empathic expression.

We have argued that a morality of the heart is best viewed within the context of empathic experience. Threaded through a heart morality are a variety of emotions that reflect personal values and one's objects of attachments (affective knowledge). Moreover, emotional and empathic expressions are integral to our lives as loving human beings. Yet such expressions do not insure a moral response. As we have seen, one can simply "wallow" in empathy, overempathize with another, or lose necessary boundaries. Moreover, emotions can blind us to the reality of a situation and be a source of denial and distortion. What is needed is some frame of reference that grounds our emotions and empathic expressions. Stated simply, what is needed is a transformation of empathic experience. It is this transformation of our empathic development that molds and shapes a response to the call of Jesus to "come and follow me" (Mark 10:21), an invitation that each Christian is invited to accept.

The Sources for Christian Empathy

A full understanding of empathy's role in our experience as Christians must incorporate dimensions that include one's relationship with the believing community as well as one's relationship with God revealed through Jesus Christ. The Letter to the Hebrews serves as a fruitful starting point. The Hebrews writer notes Jesus' solidarity with humankind primarily in terms of Jesus' own suffering. Jesus' own empathic response is pointedly reflected in three passages from this letter.

> Since he was himself tested through what he suffered, he is able to help those who are tempted (2:18).

> For we do not have a high priest who is unable to sympathize with our weakness, but one who was tempted in every way that we are, yet never sinned (4:15).

> He is able to deal patiently with erring sinners, for he himself is beset by weakness (5:2)

These passages, written to what might loosely be termed a "midlife crisis" community of weary Christians, offer encouragement by speaking of Jesus as weak and suffering. Central to the whole theme of Hebrews is Jesus the compassionate high priest, one who endured our own human impoverishment. Through this Jesus we know that we have a God who has become everything that we are and has transformed our humanness with the piercing power of his own compassionate stance through the act of complete self-donation. The thrust of these passages hinges on the dynamics of empathic experience. What the writer directly addresses is the suffering and impoverishment of God. It is the God who is suffering who is able to reach out and understand, to comfort and support us in our trials. Jesus' capacity to empathically experience our condition is what gives these passages their power and the reader hope and encouragement.

What is of consequence for a developing theory of Christian empathy is the realization that an empathic Jesus finds validation in social psychological research. Psychological studies indicate that those who have experienced the suffering and pains of others are most apt to empathize with others' misfortunes and hurts. We have noted in a previous chapter that "people frequently respond more empathically to other's experience when they themselves have had similar experiences."[12] Jesus "beset by weakness" is able to respond to our own struggles and unique predicaments. On a personal note, I am always struck at liturgical events where these passages are read by the reassuring effect they have on the congregation. Their popularity seems to arise from this rooted empathic experience. Our sufferings as humans find solace in a God who also suffers and who empathizes with our plight.

Further, this compassionate Jesus proclaims the Reign of God through a stance of loving fidelity to the Father. This Reign acknowledges the presence of God's mastery within our human history, a presence that is with us even now. This ruling presence calls for the transformation (Rom. 12:2) of our Christian existence, both personal and social, to make this Reign more real in our midst. In this context, empathic development serves as a channel for Christian praxis. Psychological research indicates a relationship between empathy and human tendencies toward altruism. We noted above that those who are suffering are more likely to empathize with others. The literature also leads us to conclude that "cumulatively," as Staub maintains, "the research findings do suggest that empathy is a likely determinant of helping."[13] The presence of empathy, therefore, fosters not only an openness and vulnerability to the hurts of others, but encourages actual behaviors that promote Christian praxis.

The reality of empathy's import, likewise, becomes clear from studying the life of St. Paul. For Paul, Christians "live in the Lord" and the distinct experience of life in Jesus Christ is made evident in the role of service or vocation to which every Christian is called. Gifts, given in the Lord (1 Cor. 2:12), are to be used to bring about the unity of the believing community. Yet Paul must exhort the Corinthian community in the proper use of these gifts. In the dispute over speaking in tongues and the dissension caused by eating the food of idols,

Paul speaks eloquently of the need to nurture behaviors and gifts that "build up" and bring unity to the community.

Two examples in 1 Corinthians point to the emphasis that Paul placed on the Corinthians' need to care for one another, which, in turn, would strengthen the community. In 1 Corinthians 8, Paul writes of the discord prevalent in the Corinthian community over the eating of meat that had been offered to idols. Some Christians had perceived no problem in eating this food, whereas others found these practices to be immoral, a judgment based largely on their preconversion upbringing, and were scandalized by those Christians who were eating such food.

How should the Christian respond in such a case? Paul saw nothing inherently wrong for the believing Christian to eat idolatrous food (1 Cor. 8:8). On the other hand, if eating this food caused a scandal among other Christians in the community, then the mature Christian was obliged to forego eating this food: "Therefore, if food causes my brother or sister to sin, I will never eat meat again, so that I may not be an occasion of sin to him or her" (1 Cor. 8:13). For Paul, then, the needs and concerns of one's fellow Christians take priority over one's own desire and preferences. In this way, the "folly" of the cross is made real when Christians surrender personal desires for the good of the community. Many would judge this surrender of personal desire to be foolish, but mature Christians realize the importance of this action for the well-being of the total community.

Paul restates his theme of "building up" in 1 Corinthians 14 when he discusses the place of "tongues" in the Corinthian church. Members of the Corinthian community had the gift of tongues and were flaunting this gift at the expense of other gifts. In fact, it appears that the entire community was guilty of placing far too much emphasis on the gift of tongues. Paul remonstrated against this inordinate emphasis on one particular gift: "Brothers and sisters, do not be childish in your outlook. Be like children as far as evil is concerned, but in mind be mature" (1 Cor. 14:20).

Paul advised the Corinthians to keep in mind the desires and needs of the entire community. A person's gifts must be seen in light of the needs of others. True Christian maturity, then, is making one's own needs secondary to the good of the community. Paul responds to this Corinthian situation by saying that all things must be done "with a constructive purpose" (1 Cor. 14:26). We see again that Paul's attention is not on the privatized good of any one person, but rather on the good of the entire community, which is paramount for Paul.

Paul saw that true maturity depended on the care and concern that Christians have for one another. Paul considers this care and concern for others indispensable for living the Christian life. From a psychological perspective, what human capacity allows one to be aware of other community members' needs and to respond in a loving manner to their concerns? The quality of community interaction that Paul wishes for the Corinthian community would remain elusive if it were not for a strong empathic bonding existing between individual members within the community.

These very concrete and human experiences of early church community building demonstrate the critical importance of an empathic sense. Paul's own struggle to encourage the Corinthians to be aware of the hurt and pain of one's brothers and sisters as well as his stress on recognizing the importance of various gifts that different community members possess bolster the need for a Christian empathic sense. For our own day, the personal interaction and social unity of any Christian community is linked together by the care, trust, and social bonding that exists among community members.

This empathic foundation of early church community building is explicit in Paul's own life. Paul's reflections intimate this empathic sense. In several key passages (1 Thess. 1:6; 2 Thess. 3:7; 1 Cor. 11:1; Gal. 4:12) in the Pauline corpus, Paul urges the Christian communities to be "imitators of me." This prompting by Paul, says David Stanley,

> springs both from Paul's apostolic authority as an authentic representative of Christian tradition, and from the recognized need of those he fathered in the faith to have an objective, concrete norm against which they can test (*dokimazein*) the influence of the Spirit upon themselves.[14]

This experience of imitating Paul, however, is far more than a learning experience — observing and modeling the actions of another. In essence, this imitation is a realization of the depth of Paul's own real suffering and the end to which his life is oriented. It is a suffering of "fellowship" borne by Paul and every Christian with Christ. This suffering, through the Spirit, unites in turn all Christians "for truly his [Paul's] own daily experience of 'dying' formed but a share of the vast suffering of Christ that all Christians, and especially apostolic laborers, must bear in order to bring the body of Christ to full measure." In other words, this deepening bond of unity with the compassionate Lord, a bond proclaimed through pastoral labors, constitutes the

Christian's own empathic sensitivity to the suffering Jesus as well as to the needs of one's brothers and sisters.

Christian Empathy and Therapeutic Empathy: A Difference

Yet we need to ask how Christian empathy differs from psychological empathy or the skills so commonly viewed as necessary for counselors and therapists. Recall from chapter 2 that, viewed therapeutically, empathy has received rich treatment from the humanistic school whose main proponent is Carl Rogers, with its stress on interpersonal communication. An analysis of this literature leads to the conclusion that therapeutic empathy has three functions: (1) correctly perceiving the client's state; (2) personally understanding this state; (3) adequately communicating a response that reflects this understanding.

Christian empathy absorbs these characteristics, yet provides more. First, Christian empathy finds inadequate a therapeutic assumption that simply acknowledges another's situation — whether it be sorrow, joy, or hurt. Christian empathy always leads the one who is empathically aroused to inquire how one's own internal state relates to and is made meaningful by the life, death, and resurrection of Jesus. "The given factor is, after all: definitive salvation-coming-from-God in Jesus of Nazareth, the crucified-and-risen One. 'It is God who delivers us in Jesus Christ' (see 2 Cor. 5:19). God saved, but in and through the man Jesus, his message, life and death."[15] Thus, the sufferings of empathic Christians are not ends in themselves; rather, they are made meaningful and intelligible through the bonding and sustaining relationship one has with others through Jesus Christ.

Additionally, the sufferings of the empathic Christian take on the perspective of Paul for "even now I find my joy in the suffering I endure for you" (Col. 1:24). Christian empathy finds its true meaning in following the self-emptying of Jesus (Phil. 2:6), in bearing patiently one's own suffering, and waiting in hopeful expectation.

> ...we even boast of our afflictions! We know that affliction makes for endurance for tested virtue, and tested virtue for hope. And this hope will not leave us disappointed, because the love of God has been poured out in our hearts through the Holy Spirit who has been given to us. (Rom. 5:3–5)

The Christian's empathic stance, which is an invitation to vulnerability and hurt, is itself a response of joy for "rejoice instead, in the measure that you share Christ's suffering" (1 Pet. 4:13).

Finally, Christian empathy goes beyond understanding and acknowledging another's pain and hurt. Christian empathy fosters a praxis orientation that seeks to alter what is contributory to current misery, suffering, and oppression. As noted above, empathy's fostering of altruistic behavior blends with the goal of the Christian life: continual self-donation in service to one's brothers and sisters.[16]

Based on the foregoing reflections, Christian empathy is defined as *the human capacity, transformed by grace, that leads to experiencing to some degree on an affective level another's situation; meaning is given to this experiencing through a personal relationship with Jesus Christ, thus motivating one to offer willingly his or her gifts, nurtured in a believing community of faith, for the building of God's Reign.*

Christian Empathy: A Further Inquiry

Greater insight into the linkage of Christian empathy and psychological research is provided by examining the Parable of the Good Samaritan (Luke 10:29–37). A lawyer inquires of Jesus, "And who is my neighbor?" Instead of answering the question directly, Jesus employs a common teaching mode, the parable. A man traveling to Jericho falls victims to robbers. They strip and beat him, leaving him for dead. Later, a priest walks by and, although seeing him, journeys on. The same fate befalls the man when a Levite passes by. A Samaritan, however, who is traveling along the road encounters the "half-dead" man and "was moved to pity [or compassion] at the sight" (10:33). The Samaritan bandages the man's wounds, helps him onto his beast, and takes him to a nearby inn. There he cares for him and, before leaving, gives the innkeeper two silver pieces, instructing him to care for the wounded traveler. Further, he promises to take care of any additional expenses the innkeeper might incur in caring for the man. After finishing the parable Jesus inquires as to which of the three men (the priest, the Levite, or the Samaritan) is "neighbor" to the man. The response is, naturally, "the one who treated him with compassion" (10:37). Upon hearing this reply, Jesus responds with an instructive message "Then go and do the same" (10:37).

Scripture scholar John Donahue's analysis of this parable offers fascinating insight into the power of empathy.[17] The victim in the parable is without an identity, a nameless individual whose journey ends in tragedy. The "shock" for the reader arises, says Donahue, when official members of the religious establishment choose not to offer aid and pass by in seeming indifference. Moreover, the one who does rescue the unfortunate victim is a member of the hated Samaritan community. In ancient times Jews felt great animosity toward their Samaritan neighbors and refused to associate with them.

> The shock of the parable is that the one who stops, who paradoxically fulfills the law, is the enemy and religious apostate. This shock challenges the hearers' understanding of God and whom God approves; it shatters a narrow interpretation of the law and unmasks the hatreds and divisions which often become institutionalized by religious strife. This parabolic paradox is parallel to the kingdom proclamation of Jesus and to his offer of God's mercy to sinners and outcasts.[18]

The power of the parable comes from the Samaritan's viewing of the injured man and his experience of compassion for him. Says Donahue:

> Compassion is that divine quality which, when present in human beings, enables them to share deeply in the sufferings and needs of others and enables them to move from one world to the other: from the world of helper to the one needing help; from the world of the innocent to that of the sinner. Under Luke's tutelage the parable becomes *a paradigm of the compassionate vision* which is the presupposition for ethical action.[19]

The true neighbor, then, is the one who shows "mercy" (10:37), identified by the Greek word *eleos*. Moreover, it is this "mercy" that allows the breaking of stereotypes and rigid categories that degrade and imprison ourselves and others. As Donahue rightly notes:

> If the injured man was a Jew, his first contact with Samaritans may have been when he awoke in the inn. His brush with death could have opened his own vision of who is neighbor and where goodness can be found.[20]

How might we link the compassionate mercy shown by the Samaritan and our psychological understanding of empathy? An answer to this question comes from an analysis of two key Greek words in the Lucan text: *splanchnizomai* and *eleos*.[21]

In Luke 10:33 we read that the traveler "was moved to pity" at the sight of the half-dead man. The Greek word for being moved to pity is *splanchnizomai*. The related noun form is *splanchna* (plural). "The *splanchna* are the entrails of the body, or as we might say today, the guts. They are the place where are most intimate and intense emotions are located."[22] Moreover, *splanchna* also refers to the seat of emotion, the "heart," or love. The *splanchna* are that which is most inward, those feelings most central to our core sense of self. The Greek word reflects a visceral arousal of significant intensity. The "pity" of the Good Samaritan reflects this physiological reaction. The Samaritan's response is at a very "gut" level. He is upset and pained at viewing the unfortunate traveler's plight and is moved to respond.

The New Testament shows this compassionate reaction to be the response of Jesus:

> When Jesus was confronted with human need, the New Testament therefore says he was moved in his bowels — i.e., he had pity and compassion (Matt. 9:36; 14:14; 20:34; 15:32; Mark 8:2; Mark 1:41; 6:34; Luke 7:13). In this sense mercy is an inner feeling. Nevertheless, it is worthy of note that such feeling in Jesus always gave rise to an outward act of succor.[23]

The *linkage* between feeling (emotional arousal) and action is critical. The life of Jesus and his use of the Good Samaritan parable demonstrate both the interior and exterior response required for the Christian life: the transformation we are called to resides both within ourselves and in responsible action for others.

The Greek word *eleos* is best translated as "mercy." Scripture provides many meanings of "mercy." In the Hebrew Bible there are Yahweh's familial love for his people and his faithful commitment to the covenant that represents his loving fidelity. In the New Testament "mercy" is shown through Jesus Christ, who invites humankind to wholeness. Jesus forgives our faults and invites us to forgive and render aid toward all, and most particularly those in need.

In Luke 10:37 we learn that one's true neighbor is one who treats others "with compassion," that is, with the *eleos* shown by the Good Samaritan. *Eleos* is the emotion that arises when we encounter another's plight and distress. It is "the divinely required attitude"[24] we must show one another. The Good Samaritan's action is the loving kindness that Jesus requires of his disciples. In essence, *eleos* becomes the criterion for evaluating whether we truly are a loving and kind people.

In sum, the mercy asked of the Christian is costly. It requires being moved and jolted. When encountering pain, suffering, or injustice the Christian cannot stand safely removed. He or she feels such pain, is moved by such reactions, and answers through responsible action.

What strikes us, though, is the remarkable similarity between compassionate mercy and the psychological understanding of empathy arising out of recent research. As we have seen in our discussion of Hoffman's theory, the empathic response is affective, cognitive, and motivational. It is a visceral response flowing from awareness of another's plight, and it invites one to purposeful action whose aim is to alleviate such pain and suffering. The compassionate mercy of the Good Samaritan is, in other words, the human response of empathy transformed by the divine attitude Jesus asks of each of us in everyday life. The response of the Samaritan was a very *human* response, yet it reflected what Jesus desires from each of us. In essence, Jesus beckons forth our very humanity to embrace compassionately this world, in order to proclaim a "wholly new realm of life, one in which this body is completely vivified by the grace of the Spirit" (Rom. 8:11).

The nature of empathy, moreover, is fundamental for Christian praxis. Throughout our discussion we have relied upon the insights of psychological research in order to probe how we do indeed respond as humans. The importance of this perspective cannot be overestimated. The Lord uses our humanity and calls for its transformation (Rom. 12:2). In the mystery of God's plan, our humanity is oriented through our empathic expressions to respond to the Lord's beckoning.

From a human perspective, empathy provides what Hoffman terms a "mature motive force"[25] that undergirds our moral action. This force is not found in the Kohlberg's cognitive account of moral development. The cognitive-developmental school is unable to explain how moral reasoning will lead to action, though, in fairness to the cognitive-developmental view, we acknowledge that research indicates that individuals with higher moral reasoning stages will often perform greater levels of moral action compared to those who reason at lower stages.[26] Nonetheless, reason simply does not translate into action. What we must ask is this: What *within human experience* allows for moral action to emerge? The question is begged in the cognitive-developmental school. The empathic arousal at another's plight and the transformation of this arousal through one's understanding of another's situation into sympathetic distress (compassion) provides the answer. One is consciously motivated to aid the other, to offer support or relief, or provide what service one can, one is moved at a visceral level, because of another's situation. Our empathic reactions serve as a motivating force for guiding our service to others. More than anything else, the beauty of the Good Samaritan parable is that the Samaritan remained, simply, *true to his humanity*. He chose not to compartmentalize his empathic reaction through ideology and religious indoctrination (as reflected by the priest and Levite), thereby blocking his arousal to the traveler's plight. On the contrary, he admitted to the truth of who he was, a human being bonded to and responsible for others within the human community.

Interestingly, psychologists have attempted to translate the Good Samaritan story into psychological research. Two psychologists who have studied extensively the psychology of helping behavior, John Darley and Daniel Batson, devised an experimental situation that replicated the Lucan parable.[27] Forty seminarians who were paid volunteers were asked to give a talk on either employment prospects for seminarians (a secular topic) or on the parable of the Good Samaritan. The seminarians were instructed to go to another building to present their talk. Half the subjects for each type of talk were told they were under time pressure and needed to leave immediately, whereas the other half were under no such time constraint. Along the way all subjects encountered a distressed person in need of help. These researchers measured two factors that might influence one's tendency to respond in an altruistic fashion. Would those who were to give a talk on the Good Samaritan be more likely to stop and help (the premise being that one's conscious values and beliefs might induce one to be more caring)? A second variable to be measured was, simply, time. Would those under time pressures be more likely to ignore the person in need? The examination of such a simple variable as time is significant. In our everyday lives it is the realities of obstacles such as "not enough time" that often influence our response. The reader might simply ask himself or herself to recall instances when he or she was rushed and failed to recognize the need of another or because of time constraints failed to do a kind deed that, given a more leisurely opportunity, he or she might have done.

Analysis of the data demonstrated that time was a significant variable in determining whether one would aid the person in distress. Thus, those under no time constraints responded significantly more often to aiding the distressed person than those under time pressures. The type of speech given, however, had no effect as to whether the seminarian helped the distressed. These researchers concluded that "thinking about the Good Samaritan did not increase helping behavior, but being in a hurry decreased it."[28]

It would be natural to assume that these seminarians held values and beliefs that were consonant with the message of the Good Samaritan parable. Nonetheless, situational pressures (e.g., time) inhibited their ability to act. A later reanalysis of the original findings, however, utilizing different statistical procedures reached a partially different conclusion.[29] This later analysis confirmed the finding of time pressure but concluded that it was highly probable that the seminarians who were to speak on the parable of the Good Samaritan were much more likely to aid the distressed person than those seminarians who were speaking on a secular topic.

The value of this research allows us to view the *complexity* of moral action. Though we have argued that empathy is integral for love and acts of care, other factors must also be taken into consideration. From a psychological perspective, to respond compassionately one must view internal psychological dynamics (e.g., empathic arousal) as well as numerous other variables. Among these other influences are a person's life history, current situational stressors, the beliefs and attitudes of the person, and the environmental situation. Communities that seek to foster care and support among their members must look to these other factors as well.

Christian Empathy: Its Application

If an understanding of Christian empathy is to be of value, then it proves helpful to address various dimensions of human living — the intrapsychic, the interpersonal, and the social. By examining each of these dimensions, we are able to ascertain the integral role that Christian empathy might exercise for various ministries.

First, our own intrapsychic experience provides several possibilities for Christian empathy's application. When we previously reflected on Christian empathy, we had noted the empathic Jesus and the compassionate stance that emerged from his own struggle and weakness. Our Christian empathy, likewise, is intimately tied to accepting our own human weakness and the depths of our own human impoverishment. Accepting our very humanness invites us to experience conversion or the radical change and transformation of ourselves in light of the Gospel message. This radical confrontation from within allows for the experience of acknowledging personal weakness, of deepening self-knowledge, and of accepting our life-suffering that in turn lead us to the Spirit that fortifies our own empathic stance. The radical challenge of conversion and the stark openness and vulnerability that empathy invites us to are mutually intertwined, and from them flow our growing solidarity with the sufferings of our brothers and sisters.

Additionally, empathy blends nicely with recent writings in ethics and spirituality that speak of the need for personal discernment. Increasingly, emphasis in spirituality focuses on deepening awareness of who we are in relation to the God who calls us. We are called to a growing awareness of and sensitivity to our affections, desires, and interior disposition. To pose the fundamental question "What is God calling me to now?" calls for a continual probing of one's self-understanding, one's surroundings, as well as the needs of one's brothers and sisters within the human community. Such awareness and sensitivity find strong support through the deepening empathic sense that fosters awareness of self, others, and the challenge of Jesus' saving message.

In the *Spiritual Exercises*, Ignatius offers a prayer experience that relies on the retreatant's ability to utilize his or her empathic sense.[30] The retreatant is invited to experience the life of Jesus — his joys, sorrows, hurts, and pains. Toward the beginning of the *Exercises*, for example, the retreatant asks for the grace "to know Jesus intimately, to love him more intensely, and so to follow him more closely." The thrust of current interest in prayer and meditation often parallels this Ignatian prayer experience of encountering personally our Lord's life and death. Such relational encounters with God are possible because of our empathic experience.

An integral part of any Christian's life is the using of one's gifts in various ministries. Such labor takes on a decidedly interpersonal dimension. Here, too, within this interpersonal context, empathy's role is of great consequence.

One of St. Ignatius's favorite Pauline texts appears in 1 Corinthians where Paul states, "I became all things to all persons so as to win all to Christ" (1 Cor. 9:22). In his own pastoral reflections Ignatius acknowledges Paul's urging:

> In dealing with men of position or influence, if you are to win their affection for the greater glory of God Our Lord, look first to their disposition and accommodate yourselves to them. If they are of a lively temper, quick and merry of speech, follow their lead in your dealing with them.[31]

At the beginning of the *Spiritual Exercises*, likewise, Ignatius notes that "it is necessary to presuppose that every good Christian is more ready to put a good interpretation on another's statement than to condemn it as false." What Ignatius envisions for ministers is a fundamental attitude of openness to and acceptance of others. Ignatius's pastoral vision is more than simply hearing the other. Ignatius invites the pastoral laborer to attempt a more profound understanding, to know a person interiorly, to understand him or her at the core level. This empathic focus of Ignatius's reflections is quite clear. It is clear, likewise, that the pastoral vision of any person using his or her gifts to "build up" the community is enhanced when that person is attentive and sensitive to the needs, desires, and internal states of the one he or she is ministering to (admittedly we are emphasizing here the therapeutic view of empathy as well as Hoffman's developmental view; both perspectives, moreover, are vital).

In a similar vein, we might ponder the interpersonal dimension as it pertains to community building. Environmental factors that nurture and sustain human growth provide viable opportunities for empathic development. Among these are focusing on the adequacy of modeling influences within the community, giving clarity to community goals, stressing issues clarification regarding the hurts and stresses of community members, encouraging competency skills that are requisite for adult ministerial roles, and creating role-taking opportunities for community members. Any Christian community would do well to consider the various social and psychological variables that influence empathy's development.

Finally, it is imperative to view empathy's role in the formation of social compassion. To consider how empathy might give meaning to the social dimension of various ministries, it is helpful to consider the Aristotelian dictum that a virtue might be known by examining its vice. What is the opposite of empathy? The word that comes to my mind is "power." But a cautionary note is warranted. Power per se is not evil. And no doubt legitimate uses of power are absolutely necessary for bringing stability and order to a complex world. The power we are examining here is the tendency to control and acquire personal gain at the expense of one's fellow humans. It is this type of power that encourages and sustains the injustice, alienation, and oppression that engulfs the world today.

In American society this power is nurtured by the "cultural addiction" of competition. Such competition is found in the academic system, the business world, our politics of government decision making, and in institutional structures.[32] It is this competitive drive, sustained in an atmosphere for power and control, that blunts and numbs our capacity to empathize with others — to be sensitive, to be open, to be vulnerable. Martin Hoffman hypothesizes that it is this very struggle — the tension that the developing child and adolescent feel between their own empathic urges and the realization of the necessity for competition and personal gain in American society — that contributes to the personal conflicts and alienation that many youth feel today.[33]

Equally important, however, is the possibility that empathy offers humankind for countering these power-based temptations. Recalling once again the words of psychologist Kenneth Clark, we can view the antidote that empathic experiences have to the power-based motives so present within society and our own lives. He notes that "the highest and probably the least frequent form of empathy is that in which the individual is compelled to embrace all human beings. . . . It is the level of empathy that religion seeks to reinforce, with varying degrees of failure."[34] In addition, he states, "it is the level of empathy that, when real and functional, can not be used to justify the naked use of power, tyranny, flagrant or subtle injustices, cruelties, sustained terrorism, killings, wars, and eventual extinction."[35] And, he observes, "this lack of simple expanded empathy is in the eyes of the observer the basis for social tension, conflicts, violence, terrorism and war."[36]

It is this empathic arousal, nurtured by modeling and supportive community environments that articulate valued stances, that offers the optimum strategy for fostering social compassion. Moreover, it is precisely this empathic component of a social compassion orientation that enables one to respond to the question, "Lord when did we see you hungry and feed you or see you thirsty and give you drink?" (Matt. 25:37). It is an empathic response, nurtured in a relationship with Jesus and one's Christian community, that provides the capacity to respond to the very hunger and thirst so necessary for building God's Reign here and now.

As a way to sum up Christian empathy's applications, we might, for example, imagine a world where parish congregations and ministers feel, experience, and are aware of the needs and hurts of one another. We might consider a school where students can feel the interest of their teachers and where instructors are aware of and sensitive to the needs of their students. Or we might ponder a country where its leaders and elected officials empathize with the human hurt, the poverty, the unemployment, and human despair of their citizens. These concrete reflections teach us the fruitfulness of an empathic perspective for our Christian lives.

Finally, the perspective of Christian empathy offers the possibility of newer insights for theological understanding and ministerial insight. One question that the perspective of Christian empathy might lead us to consider is how an empathic perspective contributes to the social bonding and attachment that communities need in order to survive. In an age of increasing specialization and pluralism, this question emerges as a crucial focus for the building of community. Religious educators might address opportunities in the curriculum and environmental concerns that foster and stimulate empathic development. Likewise, ministry specialists might ponder what role empathy has in the forming of pastoral skills and human relationship building. There are numerous related issues that might be explored. How might empathy influence one's ministerial style? What role and what form does empathy take in the assessment of basic ministerial competency?

➤ *Chapter 6* ◄

Living the Heart:
Some Pastoral Reflections

For I know well the plans I have in mind for you, says the Lord, plans for your welfare, not for woe! plans to give you a future full of hope. When you call me, when you go to pray to me, you will find me. Yes, when you seek me with all your heart, you will find me with you, says the Lord, and I will change your lot.
— Jeremiah 29:11–14

Over the previous chapters we have established the significance of a heart morality consonant with the Christian moral vision. Moreover, we do not dismiss the rational side of morality; indeed, it remains vital for any moral discussion. Yet, as we have tried to show, when addressing moral concerns, we have given far too little attention to the affective side of human experience.

I do not believe either moral perspective alone is adequate to address the numerous personal and social problems that humans encounter. We need to view the importance of both perspectives in moral discussion. Psychologist Jerome Kagan frames well the need for both perspectives:

Perhaps each of us is persuaded of the moral rightness of an idea by two different, incommensurate processes. One is based on feelings; the other, on logical consistency with a few deep premises. When a standard derives its strength from either foundation, we find it difficult to be disloyal to its directives. When it enjoys the support of both, as it does for torture and unprovoked murder, its binding force is maximal.[1]

117

To illustrate the above, the reader might pause for a moment and ask the question: Whom have I considered the "moral heroes" in my life? If we recall such people and reflect on their lives, we are apt to find that they embrace both the cognitive and affective dimensions we have stressed. That is, they are people who hold deeply to a set of beliefs. Equally important, they are people who feel deeply about such beliefs. Their emotions energize their moral thought, giving it a power unavailable from thinking alone.

Further, we must readily acknowledge the weakness of both perspectives, for any morality is apt to lead one to be short-sighted if its limits are not understood. "It is important that we assess the merits and demerits of a love or altruism rationale against those of justice structures. Just as altruism may have difficulty resolving conflicts of interest, justice may have difficulty (if it has anything to say at all) prescribing ideals of character and community)."[2] I do believe, though, that in the daily living of life the heart approach we have set forth appears more able to embrace everyday moral concerns and so sculpt our own moral identity. Awareness of our empathic yearnings, reflection on our emotional attachments, as well as serious scrutiny given to such psychic processes as the dimensions of conscience outlined in chapter 4 (e.g., probing our use of defense mechanisms) are essential for fostering moral growth. Indeed, the advantage of a heart morality is that it appears to resonate with people's human experience. Whereas the moral reasoning of Kohlberg's dilemmas is provocative, it remains far removed from everyday life. In other words, my suspicion is that moral development is most apt to occur if we focus on what makes sense to us as humans. The heart morality we have set forth offers the best hope for moral development because it expresses what being human is really all about. Simply stated, it makes sense; it is *who we are*, it reflects what we experience as we struggle to fashion and live the moral life. I would also submit that if we want to encourage moral growth in others, we need to address what they experience in their daily life. This is especially significant in the moral guidance we offer youth. If we can help them to examine their attachments and encourage their empathic expressions we foster what is vital and at the very core of their life. It is an investment that we as adults can ill afford not to make.

It must be stated that arriving at a moral decision is a complex process to which a heart morality offers only a perspective. Moreover, for any Christian, formulating a moral response requires dialogue with the traditions and beliefs of his or her community of faith. Having said this, I do believe, though, there are some common insights that can be gathered from reflecting on the heart perspective we have offered that provide deepening self-insight and possibilities for moral growth and that can be of aid to us in both our own lives and in various ministries and pastoral practice. I would like to discuss some of these possibilities below, drawing on my own clinical and pastoral experience as well as on insights of psychology.

The Role of Gratitude

Gratitude offers a particularly powerful means to deal with the hurt and anger that often afflict our lives. Several months ago I was going through a personal crisis. As a way to cope with this crisis I kept in regular contact with several friends. At the end of one conversation, one friend said to me, "Remember, Charlie, no matter what happens, God loves you." I thanked my friend for this comment, though at the moment I did not consider it further. Later that evening, however, in prayer, those three words, "God loves you" became pivotal. After repeating those words several times in my mind I was drawn to an overwhelming sense of God's love. For a brief period the anger, hurt, and self-pity I was feeling began to recede. I was allowed a "new way of seeing." A stream of feelings and memories soon crossed my mind. I felt a great sense of the "consolation of my life history" as I reflected upon and felt the numerous times God had cared for me and shown me love.[3] No longer was I simply a prisoner of my negativity; a freeing sense of God's peace and gratefulness became the filters through which I began to interpret the recent events of my life. Being a Jesuit, I was led to the *Spiritual Exercises*, going through those known as the "First Week."[4] I confronted both my own sin and my psychological vulnerabilities and began to understand how they coalesced to frustrate within me a free response to the Lord.

What transpired over the next few months was an intense struggle. My own darkness, manifested through wounded self-esteem and self-pity led me to interpret my life history and my current situation in ways leading to narrowing attitudes, hardened feelings, and emotional upset. Fortunately, the sense of gratitude gradually prevailed. Though still able to recognize my legitimate hurt and anger, I found that with time my "eyes were opened," the darkness that for months had colored my life slowly evaporated. I felt truly loved, indeed someone "special" in God's eyes. God had radically touched my life. My own sin and limitations showed me what I truly meant to God; in essence, it was through my sin and vulnerabilities that I found reconciliation. I found myself relishing the words of Paul: "I thank Christ Jesus our

Lord, who has strengthened me, that he has made me his servant and judged me faithful. I was once a blasphemer, a persecutor, a man filled with arrogance; but because I did not know what I was doing in my unbelief, I have been treated mercifully, and the grace of our Lord has been granted me in overflowing measure, along with the faith and love that are in Christ Jesus" (1 Tim. 12–15). The resulting fruit of such gratitude was a deepening freedom and desire to serve the Lord.

In chapter 3 we noted the power that negative feelings have over our lives. Often we do become prisoners to such feelings whose end result is literally to hold us hostage, thereby preventing us from viewing a wider moral vision or other perspectives. Yet, there is hope.

Though we are all held captive at times by negative emotions, they need not imprison us. We can actively counter this tendency, though it takes *effort*. We can channel our energies into recalling positive experiences, moments of satisfaction and joy, and instances of serenity and peace. Imprisonment by negative feelings

> can be counteracted by constantly being aware of how fortunate one's condition is and of how it could have been otherwise, or actually was otherwise before — by rekindling impact through recollection and imagination. Enduring happiness seems possible, and it can be understood theoretically. However, note that it does not come naturally by itself. It takes effort.[5]

Imaginatively experiencing times of being loved by others, and particularly by the Lord who gave his life, provides a needed antidote to the all too common tendency to harbor negative feelings. When one experiences gratitude, one experiences that he or she is valued and accepted. "This is especially the case where any measure of sacrifice or concession or consideration is shown; he has been willing to incur a sacrifice of his own convenience or welfare to assist me. This shows that my welfare is valued by him in addition to his own. I am an object of his concern."[6] My own healing took place through this realization. Though hurting deeply, I was able through the Lord's help to recount his love for me by his own self-sacrifice. From this realization I felt valued, I felt loved.

"The sorts of feelings and attitudes involved in gratitude *do* play an important role in our moral life."[7] In essence, the experience of gratitude orients us morally, for gratitude involves respect and concern for others as well as relationship with them. Gratitude conveys thought and feeling:

Gratitude shows the role of the affective life in morality in an especially cogent way.... Among the feelings and attitudes expressed in gratitude are those of appreciation of the other person and one's attitude of respect for the other person as someone of value in himself, and not merely as the source of one's own welfare. Having this kind of regard, taking these attitudes toward others is essentially involved in having a morality. Those with whom we share moral relations are not merely creatures whose behavior exhibits certain patterns but whose behavior manifests attitudes of valuing, respect, and concern.[8]

In sum, the experience of gratitude provides a rich resource for undoing the shackles of negativity that bind us.

Of all feelings, perhaps none is so able to frustrate growth in the moral life as much as anger. When angry we become distracted from our moral vision. We experience upset and focus our attention on the source of the anger. Though this is understandable and at times necessary, particularly when questions of justice are involved or unwarranted deep hurt arises, such angry feelings can derail us from attending to other necessary tasks and eclipse the moral vision we seek to embrace.

In order to counter such negative self-absorption, not to mention the preoccupation with the source of our anger, it is important to call attention to our desires. I often ask those who are angry (after a thorough discussion of the situation that led to the anger) what they really desire. I explore with them their core values. By no means do I attempt to dismiss the extraordinary hurt one might feel, but at some point such feelings must be reconciled with *who we are*, that is, *a person of the heart.* Some key questions I have found helpful for myself personally and in my work with others are the following:

1. What part do I play in the hurt, disappointment, or the misunderstanding that has taken place? In other words, to what extent can I allow myself to take responsibility for what has happened?

2. Do I really understand the other person's situation and point of view?

3. Can I pray for this person?

4. If necessary, can I pray for the grace to forgive this person?

5. If my feelings are such that I cannot now pray for this person, can I pray for the grace to "desire" to pray?

6. Even if most of the misunderstanding is not mine, can I still "desire" the graces that allow for forgiveness and not become a prisoner to negativity, cynicism and bitterness?

7. Can I express my anger in an appropriate fashion — not deny-ing it, yet not letting it take root in ways that drown the desires of my heart?

The Unlimited Capacity for Blindness

Emotions such as anger (or even intense emotional states like those found in romantic infatuation) are not the only sources of our blind-ness. As we have seen, our psyche's possess the capacity to keep from awareness the true gravity of our actions or the need to take moral responsibility for what has taken place. We have labeled these pro-cesses defense mechanisms. Because defense mechanisms are by their nature unconscious (which provides them with their key for working so well), one cannot simply recognize their operations in our everyday life. Nonetheless, careful scrutiny can foster a deepening self-honesty when we evaluate our moral decisions, particularly actions that affect others in some way or that might reflect on our own self-esteem.[9]

Some of the questions below might prove helpful in providing greater awareness regarding the psyche's role in our moral lives.

Minimization. Could my action be more serious than I make it out to be? Are there any ways I am downplaying what is going on?

Denial. How open am I to receiving other's input or a differing perspective from the one I believe to be true? A rule of thumb I find helpful here is that the less capable one is of receiving input from others, the more one needs to explore what really is at issue in the decision.

Distortion. As with denial, distortion is best handled by seeking the perspectives of others.

Rationalization. What are the "reasons" why? After asking this ask yourself: "What are the *real* reasons why? If one feels a sense of discrepancy, it is worth exploring. Or, simply (and a little less threat-ening), I wonder if there might be additional reasons?

Externalization. The most helpful focus here is to reflect on the nature of responsibility and simply ask oneself: To what degree might I take responsibility? The word "degree" is important. Often if posed in dichotomous language, i.e., "you" or "me" we tend to avoid re-sponsibility. On the other hand, if we can perceive an interpersonal conflict or a situation involving someone else in terms of both par-ties (or multiple parties) as having responsibility (which is usually the case), then we can allow the word "degree" to be the frame through which we take responsibility for our action.

Inhibition. Can we risk? What might be the fears that imprison us?

Acting Out. Can I hold back? Must I act? Where is the role of reflection in my life?

Compartmentalization. What areas of my life seem to get the least self-examination (e.g., vocational, sexual). When someone I trust questions me regarding my life, in which areas do I experience the most unease or defensiveness?

Idealization. How realistic am I about my self, my situation? Do I invest qualities or attributes in others that are beyond them? Do I expect more from others than they can possibly give? Do I find myself never satisfied with some people or situations? If so, what might this say about my tendency to idealize?

Stereotyping. Can I appreciate the novel? Can other people or situations be different from my set conceptions of them? How do I react when something is different?

Educating the Emotions

Our affective lives have often been ill served; there remains the fact that our emotions are often misdirected. We have noted our emotions can energize our moral actions and display our valued concerns. Yet cultural lures easily distort emotions. Consider how loosely we speak of the emotion "love": "I 'love' that ball team." "I 'love' pretzels." Philosopher Lawrence Hinman pinpoints the essence of this aberration. I quote him at length to highlight the warping of emotion that has taken place:

> We must recognize that we are beginning with emotions which have been significantly deformed in our own society. Here the influence of advertising is of the utmost importance, for it has had a deep and pervasive influence on our emotions. Joy, one of the most important of human emotions, has become associated with a dishwashing liquid. Happiness is the feeling you get when successfully preventing a waxy build-up on your floors. Feelings of friendship come from buying Löwenbrau beer. The feeling one gets on the first real day of spring is now tied up with a menthol cigarette. The feeling of freedom is now the feeling of drinking a Pepsi without caffeine. Important emotions are connected, time after time, with inappropriate objects or actions. This cannot help but create a very basic confusion for many of us at the level of our feelings, a confusion which leads us to buy beer when we want friendship, Pepsi when we want freedom, and cigarettes when we want a new season. Part of the task of

educating the moral emotions involves freeing them from the distortions to which they have been subjected in contemporary advertising.[10]

In other words, we need to scrutinize the "ends" to which our emotions are directed. This phenomenon of misguided emotion is particularly problematic for the young. Often self-absorbed and sensitive to the felt intensity so often a part of the adolescent experience, youth become lost in the midst of their developmental needs, thereby losing awareness of the direction their emotions are leading them.

One place to begin this scrutiny is, again, to reflect on our desires. What, indeed, are our deepest desires? What do we value most? Why do we say this? What do our desires say about ourselves as moral persons? How do they reflect who we truly are? To be sure, there are many instances when we have conflicting desires. Nonetheless, probing our desires leads us to examine which desires are most central for our self-definitions as moral persons. Desires are threaded with emotion. As is often the case, emotions energize the desires that are directed toward some stated purpose or end. In this regard, we might consider the "quality" of these emotions. That is, do they lead to other-centeredness or self-absorption? Do they foster sensitivity or make us blind?

The Limits of Empathy

In our discussion we have spoken of empathy as the foundation for a heart morality. We have also made reference, however, to some problems with empathy. For ministers and professional care givers one issue that requires continual monitoring is the tendency to over-empathize, to become overinvolved in the distress or predicament of another. A problem immediately flowing from such overinvolvement is loss of objectivity. A helpful question to keep in mind in this regard is simply: Where are my boundaries? Am I capable of developing adequate boundaries in my work? An appropriate sense of boundary is necessary both in ongoing relationships with people as well as in our overall approach to work.

A second concern with empathy is the issue of becoming empathically overaroused. Such overarousal can lead to burnout and gradual shutting down in our capacity to respond to others. There does exist something that, for lack of a better term, I refer to as "healthy selfishness." For example, if parents are unwilling to care adequately for themselves they will inevitably find that their parenting abilities suffer. Not only must we create boundaries, but also periods for rest and personal nourishment. We are most apt to be able to respond empathically and appropriately when aware of our own needs and limits.

Conclusion

We have provided through our examination of empathy a viable foundation for morality rooted within human experience that is consonant with the Christian moral vision. The future challenge of empathy is, ultimately, the future hope for all — to create a world where women and men can be bonded together in love and care for one another. With Paul we realize that the focus of Christian empathy is at one with our Christian lives, which is, simply "that in any and every way...Christ is being proclaimed" (Phil. 1:19).

Notes

Chapter 1 — Reconsidering Morality: A Personal Perspective

1. Quoted in Robert Coles, *The Moral Life of Children* (Boston: Houghton Mifflin Co., 1986), 16.
2. See Charles M. Shelton, *Morality and the Adolescent* (New York: Crossroad, 1989).
3. Jerome Kagan, *The Nature of the Child* (New York: Basic Books, 1984), xiv. I would prefer to substitute the word "conscience" for "superego."
4. Norma Haan, Eliane Aerts, and Bruce A. B. Cooper, *On Moral Grounds: The Search for Practical Morality* (New York: New York University Press, 1985), 48.
5. Quoted in John L. Elias, *Moral Education: Secular and Religious* (Malabar, Fla.: Robert E. Krieger, 1989), xii.

Chapter 2 — The Kohlberg Legacy

1. Nicholas Colangelo, "Special Focus on Moral Development," *Elementary School Guidance and Counseling* 19 (1985): 244.
2. Norma Haan, Eliane Aerts, and Bruce A. B. Cooper, *On Moral Grounds: The Search for Practical Morality* (New York: New York University Press, 1985), 38.
3. Norma Haan, "Can Research on Morality Be Scientific?" *American Psychologist* 37 (1982): 1096.
4. Kenneth L. Woodward and Mary Lord, "Moral Education," *Newsweek* March 1, 1976, 74–75.
5. Lawrence Kohlberg, *The Philosophy of Moral Development* (New York: Harper & Row, 1981), 2.
6. Ibid., 105.
7. Lawrence Kohlberg, *The Psychology of Moral Development* (New York: Harper & Row, 1984), 248.
8. Lawrence Kohlberg, "Education, Moral Development, and Faith," *Journal of Moral Education* 4 (October 1974): 5.
9. Robert Kegan, *The Evolving Self* (Cambridge, Mass.: Harvard University Press, 1982), 36.

10. Richard A. Shweder, Manamohan Mahapatra, and Joan G. Miller, "Culture and Moral Development," in *The Emergence of Morality in Young Children*, Jerome Kagan and Sharon Lamb, eds. (Chicago: University of Chicago Press, 1987), 10.

11. Lawrence Kohlberg, "The Cognitive Developmental Approach to Moral Education," *Phi Delta Kappa* 56 (1975): 671. It should be pointed out that in his revisions Kohlberg has added "A" and "B" substages for each of the empirically derived stages. Individuals who demonstrate reasoning at substage B levels tend to be more autonomous and responsible in their thinking and are more inclined to view the importance of justice operations such as equality and reciprocity. For a more detailed discussion of this issue see *The Psychology of Moral Development*.

Kohlberg renamed his stages in later writings. The new terms for his more recent formulation are: Stage One: Heteronomous Morality; Stage Two: Individualistic Instrumental Morality; Stage Three: Interpersonally Normative Morality; Stage Four: Social Systems Morality; Stage Five: Human Rights and Social Welfare Morality; Stage Six: Morality of Universalizable, Reversible, and Prescriptive General Ethical Principles. See *The Psychology of Moral Development* for a discussion of his recent research.

12. Lawrence Blum, "Particularity and Responsiveness," in *The Emergence of Morality in Young Children*, 307-8.

13. Lawrence Kohlberg, "The Just Community Approach to Moral Education in Theory and Practice," *Moral Education: Theory and Application*, Marvin W. Berkowitz and Fritz Ozer, eds. (Hillsdale, N.J.: Lawrence Erlbaum, 1988), 27-87.

14. Kohlberg, *The Philosophy of Moral Development*, 182.

15. See Charles M. Shelton, *Morality and the Adolescent: A Pastoral Psychology Approach* (New York: Crossroad, 1989).

16. For a devastating critique of Kohlberg's early work see Richard A. Shweder, review of *The Philosophy of Moral Development*, by Lawrence Kohlberg, *Contemporary Psychology* 27 (1982): 421-24. For a critique of his revised work see separate reviews of *The Psychology of Moral Development*: William Damon and Raymond Montemayor, *Contemporary Psychology* 30 (1985): 952-54.

17. Kohlberg, *The Psychology of Moral Development*, 493.

18. See Susanne Villenave-Cremer and Lutz H. Eckensberger, "The Role of Affective Processes in Moral Judgment Performance," in *Moral Education: Theory and Application*, 179.

19. Kohlberg, *The Psychology of Moral Development*, 271.

20. James R. Rest, "Morality," in *Handbook of Child Psychology*, vol. 3, Paul Mussen, ed. (New York: John Wiley, 1983), 583.

21. Kohlberg, *The Psychology of Moral Development*, 249.

22. Ibid., 306.

23. Haan et al., *On Moral Grounds*, 19.

24. John C. Gibbs and Steven V. Schnell, *American Psychologist* 40 (1985): 1075.

25. James S. Leming, "Intrapersonal Variations in Stages of Moral Reasoning among Adolescents as a Function of Situational Context," *Journal of Youth and Adolescence* 7 (1978): 405–16.

26. For a discussion of the issue of ego defensiveness and morality see Haan et al., *On Moral Grounds*, and Villenave-Cremer and Eckensberger, "The Role of Affective Processes in Moral Judgment Performance."

27. Kohlberg, *The Psychology of Moral Development*, 306.

28. Carol Gilligan, *In a Different Voice* (Cambridge, Mass.: Harvard University Press, 1982), 100.

29. Colleen Cordes, "'Feminine' Morality Ignored by Theorists," *APA Monitor*, October 1984, 23.

30. Anne Colby and William Damon, review of *In a Different Voice*, by Carol Gilligan, *Merrill-Palmer Quarterly* 29: 473.

31. Ibid., 476.

32. Kohlberg, *The Psychology of Moral Development*, 360.

33. Colby and Damon, review of *In a Different Voice*, 479.

34. Carol Gilligan and Grant Wiggens, "The Origins of Morality in Early Childhood Relationships," in *The Emergence of Morality in Young Children*, Jerome Kagan and Sharon Lamb, eds. (Chicago: University of Chicago Press, 1987), 277–305. Gilligan continues to offer stimulating insights with her ongoing research. See Carol Gilligan, Janie Victoria Ward, and Jill McLean Taylor, eds., *Mapping the Moral Domain* (Cambridge, Mass.: Harvard University Press, 1988).

35. Ibid., 303.

36. Kohlberg, *The Psychology of Moral Development*, 358.

37. Ibid., 142–43.

38. Ibid., 143.

39. Ibid., 175.

40. Ibid., 141.

41. Michael S. Pritchard, "Cognition and Affect in Moral Development: A Critique of Lawrence Kohlberg," *Journal of Value Inquiry* 18 (1981): 35–49.

42. Haan et al., *On Moral Grounds*, 147.

43. Villenave-Cremer and Eckensberger, "The Role of Affective Processes in Moral Judgment Performance," 176.

44. Kohlberg, *The Psychology of Moral Development*, 293.

45. Kohlberg, *The Philosophy of Moral Development*, 300.

46. Kohlberg, "Moral Education Reappraised," *Humanist*, November/December 1978, 14.

47. Ibid.

48. Kohlberg, *The Psychology of Moral Development*, 227.

49. Douglas Hand, "Morality Lessons? Hear! Hear!" *New York Times*, April 9, 1989.

50. Jerome Kagan, "The Character of Education and the Education of Character," *Daedalus* 110 (Summer 1981): 144.

51. Ibid., 163.

52. John Philippe Rushton, *Altruism, Socialization and Society* (Englewood Cliffs, N.J.: Prentice-Hall, 1980), 64.

53. Ibid., 84.

54. Montemayor, review of *The Psychology of Moral Development*, 954.

Chapter 3 — Empathy: Morality's Heart

1. Quoted in Susanna McBee, "Morality," *U.S. News and World Report*, December 9, 1985, 58.

2. McBee, "Morality," 52–58, and Lucia Solorzano, "Rights, Wrongs: Now Schools Teach Them," *U.S. News and World Report*, May 13, 1985, 51.

3. See McBee, "Morality," 52–58; Solorzano, "Rights, Wrongs," 51; and James Hassett, "But That Would Be Wrong," *Psychology Today*, November 1981, 34–50.

4. Quoted in McBee, "Morality," 55.

5. Nicholas Colangelo and David F. Detterman, "Characteristics of Moral Problems and Solutions Formed by Students in Grades 5–8," *Elementary School Guidance and Counseling* 19 (1985): 260–71; Nicholas Colangelo, "Characteristics of Moral Problems as Formulated by Gifted Adolescents," *Journal of Moral Education*, 11 (1982): 219–32; and Stephen R. Yussen, "Characteristics of Moral Dilemmas Written by Adolescents," *Developmental Psychology* 13 (1977): 162–63.

6. Colangelo and Detterman, "Characteristics of Moral Problems and Solutions," 270.

7. *Merchant of Venice*, act 3, lines 48–62.

8. Gerald Grant, "The Character of Education and the Education of Character," *Daedalus* 110 (1981): 146.

9. Ibid.

10. Ibid., 147.

11. Ibid., 148.

12. Jerome Kagan, "The Moral Function of the School," *Daedalus* 110 (1981): 163.

13. Alasdair MacIntyre, *After Virtue* (Notre Dame, Ind.: University of Notre Dame Press, 1981), 235.

14. Robert M. Bellah, Richard Madsen, William M. Sullivan, Ann Swidler, Steven M. Tipton, *Habits of the Heart* (Berkeley: University of California Press, 1985), 76.

15. Ibid., 150–51.

16. Ibid., 50.

17. Ibid., 302.

18. Robert Hogan, "Moral Conduct and Moral Character: A Psychological Perspective," *Psychological Bulletin* 79 (1973): 222.

19. For a historical discussion of this issue see Arnold Goldstein and Gerald Y. Michaels, *Empathy Development, Training, and Consequences* (Hillsdale, N.J.: Lawrence Erlbaum, 1985), 1-11; Lauren Wispé, "History of the Concept of Empathy," in *Empathy and Its Development*, Nancy Eisenberg and Janet Strayer, eds. (New York: Cambridge University Press, 1987), 17-37.

20. Wispé, "History of the Concept of Empathy," 21.

21. Arnold Buchheimer, "The Development of Ideas about Empathy," *The Journal of Counseling Psychology* 10 (1963): 63. Quoted in Goldstein and Michaels, *Empathy Development*, 7.

22. Carl Rogers, "A Theory of Therapy, Personality, and Interpersonal Relationships as Developed in the Client-centered Framework," in *Psychology: A Study of a Science. Study I. Conceptual and Systematic*, vol. 3., *Formulations of the Person and the Social Context*, ed. S. Koch (New York: McGraw Hill, 1959), 210. Quoted in Harold Hackney, "The Evolution of Empathy," *Personnel and Guidance Journal* 57 (1978): 36.

23. Hackney, "The Evolution of Empathy," 36-37.

24. Ibid., 35.

25. Goldstein and Michaels, *Empathy Development*, 1-7.

26. For the discussion of Martin Hoffman's view of empathy and its development I rely upon the following sources from Hoffman (listed in chronological order of publication): Martin L. Hoffman, "Developmental Synthesis of Affect and Cognition and Its Implications for Altruistic Motivation," *Developmental Psychology* 11 (1975): 607-22; "Sex Differences in Empathy and Related Behaviors," *Psychological Bulletin* 84 (1977): 712-22; "Moral Development in Adolescence," in *Handbook of Adolescent Psychology*, Joseph Adelson, ed. (New York: John Wiley, 1980), 295-343; "Development of Moral Thought, Feeling, and Behavior," *American Psychologist* 34 (1979): 958-66; "Is Altruism Part of Human Nature?" *Journal of Personality and Social Psychology* 40 (1981): 121-37; "The Development of Empathy," in *Altruism and Helping Behavior*, J. Philippe Rushton and Richard M. Sorrentino, eds. (Hillsdale, N.J.: Lawrence Erlbaum, 1981), 41-63; "Development of Prosocial Motivation: Empathy and Guilt," in *The Development of Prosocial Behavior*, Nancy Eisenberg, ed. (New York: Academic Press, 1982), 281-313; "Interaction of Affect and Cognition in Empathy," in *Emotions, Cognition, and Behavior*, Carroll E. Izard, Jerome Kagan, and Robert R. Zajonc, eds. (New York: Cambridge University Press, 1984), 103-31; "Empathy, Its Limitations, and Its Role in a Comprehensive Moral Theory," in *Morality, Moral Behavior, and Moral Development*, William M. Kurtines and Jacob L. Gewirtz, eds. (New York: John Wiley, 1984), 283-302; "The Contribution of Empathy to Justice and Moral Judgment," in *Empathy and Its Development*, Nancy Eisenberg and Janet Strayer, eds. (New York: Cambridge University Press, 1987), 47-80.

27. See Hoffman, "Developmental Synthesis," 607-22, and "Is Altruism

Part of Human Nature?" 121–37. At this point in our discussion it is important to clarify the two most commonly used words in the psychological literature that are associated with care for others: "prosocial" and "altruism." The psychological literature usually delineates these two terms in the following way. "Prosocial" is used when the behavioral act benefits another, although the person might receive some reward for his or her action. On the other hand, "altruism" is used for those acts that are done selflessly and from which one derives no benefit to speak of. In fact, one might actually suffer (self-sacrifice) or encounter some personal risk when engaging in the act. There is, of course, a fine line between these two terms and the research literature reflects this thinking. For the sake of variety, the terms "prosocial," "altruistic," and "care" will be used interchangeably in our discussion. In essence, these three words will refer to a selfless orientation by one who genuinely desires to help the other, even if the behavior means some form of personal sacrifice.

28. Hoffman, "Is Altruism Part of Human Nature?" 124.

29. Paul D. MacLean, "New Findings Relevant to the Evolution of Psychosexual Function of the Brain," *Journal of Nervous and Mental Disease* 135 (1962): 289–301.

30. Ibid., 300.

31. Hoffman, "Developmental Synthesis," 610.

32. Daniel Goleman, "The Roots of Empathy Are Traced to Infancy," *New York Times*, March 28, 1989.

33. Leslie Brothers, "A Biological Perspective on Empathy," *American Journal of Psychiatry* 146 (1989): 19.

34. Hoffman, "The Contribution of Empathy," 48.

35. Ibid., 49.

36. John Cheever, "Christmas Is a Sad Season for the Poor," in *The Stories of John Cheever* (New York: Ballantine Books, 1980), 154–55.

37. Ibid., 160.

38. Hoffman, "The Development of Empathy," 45.

39. Ibid.

40. Ibid., 46.

41. Brian O'Connell, "Already 1,000 Points of Lights," *New York Times*, January 25, 1989.

42. Sarah Lyall, "Taking Solace in the Caring of Strangers," *New York Times*," January 1, 1989.

43. Hoffman, "The Development of Empathy," 47.

44. Ervin Staub, *Positive Social Behavior and Morality*, vol. 1, *Social and Personal Influences* (New York: Academic Press, 1978), 146.

45. Ibid., 148.

46. J. Philippe Rushton, "The Altruistic Personality," in *Altruism and Helping Behavior*, J. Philippe Rushton and Richard M. Sorrentino, eds. (Hillsdale, N.J.: Lawrence Erlbaum, 1981), 251–66.

47. See, for example, Nancy Eisenberg, ed. *The Development of Prosocial Behavior* (New York: Academic Press, 1982).

48. Nancy Eisenberg, "The Development of Reasoning Regarding Prosocial Behavior," in *The Development of Prosocial Behavior*, Eisenberg, ed., 241.

49. Hoffman, "Development of Prosocial Motivation," 310.

50. Goldstein and Michaels, "Empathy Development," 16.

51. "Person permanence" refers to the infant's capacity to be aware that a person exists even if not perceived. Before the infant acquires this ability, the response of the infant reflects the attitude "out of sight, out of mind."

52. Hoffman, "The Contribution of Empathy," 52.

53. Hoffman, "The Development of Empathy," 50.

54. Ibid., 51.

55. Hoffman, "Empathy, Its Limitations," 287.

56. Donald McNeill, Douglas A. Morrison, and Henri J. Nouwen, *Compassion: A Reflection on the Christian Life* (Garden City, N.Y.: Image Books, 1983), 4.

57. Ibid.

58. Richard Taylor, "Compassion," in *Vice and Virtue in Everyday Life*, Christina Hoff Sommers, ed. (San Diego: Harcourt Brace Jovanovich, 1985), 50.

59. Ibid., 47.

60. Hoffman, "Development of Prosocial Motivation," 299.

61. Ibid., 300.

62. Hoffman, "The Development of Empathy," 59.

63. Hoffman, "Is Altruism Part of Human Nature?" 134.

64. Ibid.

65. Hoffman, "Sex Differences in Empathy," 712–22.

66. Nancy Eisenberg and Randy Lennon, "Sex Differences in Empathy and Related Capacities," *Psychological Bulletin* 94, 100–131.

67. Ibid., 126.

68. Randy Lennon and Nancy Eisenberg, "Gender and Age Differences in Empathy and Sympathy," in *Empathy and Its Development*, Nancy Eisenberg and Janet Strayer, eds. (New York: Cambridge University Press, 1987), 203.

69. See Hoffman, "Empathy, Its Limitations," and "The Contribution of Empathy," for a further discussion of this issue.

70. Robert Hogan, "Moral Conduct," 224.

71. Hoffman, "The Contribution of Empathy," 75–76.

Chapter 4 — Toward a Morality of the Heart

1. Lawrence Hinman, "Emotion, Morality, and Understanding," in *Moral Dilemmas*, Carol Harding, ed. (Chicago: Precedent Publishing Co., 1985), 64.

2. Ibid., 67.

3. William C. Spohn, "The Reasoning Heart: An American Approach to Christian Discernment," *Theological Studies* 44 (1983): 31.

4. Hans Walter Wolff, *Anthology of the Old Testament* (Philadelphia: Fortress, 1973), 40–41.

5. Ibid., 40–44.

6. See Karl Rahner, "'Behold This Heart!': Preliminaries to a Theology of Devotion to the Sacred Heart," *Theological Investigations*, vol. 3 (New York: Seabury Press, 1974), 321–30; and "The Theological Meaning of the Veneration of the Sacred Heart," *Theological Investigations*, vol. 7 (New York: Seabury Press, 1977), 217–28.

7. Rahner, "'Behold This Heart!'" 329–30.

8. Karl Rahner, "Some Theses for a Theology of Devotion to the Sacred Heart," *Theological Investigations*, vol. 3 (New York: The Seabury Press, 1974), 332.

9. Kenneth B. Clark, "Empathy: A Neglected Topic in Psychological Research," *American Psychologist* 35 (1980): 189–90.

10. Richard Taylor, "Compassion," in *Vice and Virtue in Everyday Life*, Christina Hoff Sommers, ed. (San Diego: Harcourt, Brace, Jovanovich, 1985), 47–48.

11. At the same time it needs pointing out that experiences we recall are a double-edged sword. That is, for a person who experiences unhealthy guilt, such recollections can foster a crippling, intropunitive state.

12. Taylor, "Compassion," 51.

13. Jerome Kagan, *The Nature of the Child* (New York: Basic Books, 1984), 123.

14. Ibid.

15. Ben-Ami Scharfstein, "Adolescents as Philosophers: A Word in Favor of Both," in *Adolescent Psychiatry*, vol. 6, Sherman C. Feinstein and Peter L. Giovacchini, eds. (Chicago: University of Chicago Press, 1978), 51–58.

16. For a discussion of some of the commonplace processing errors, I rely on Dennis C. Turk and Peter Salovey, eds., *Reasoning, Inference, and Judgment in Clinical Psychology* (New York: Free Press, 1988).

17. Shelly E. Taylor and Jonathan D. Brown, "Illusion and Well-Being: A Social Psychological Perspective on Mental Health," *Psychological Bulletin* 103 (1988): 204.

18. Lynn H. Arnoult and Craig A. Anderson, "Identifying and Reducing Causal Reasoning Biases in Clinical Psychology," in *Reasoning, Inference, and Judgment in Clinical Psychology*, 214.

19. Norma Haan, Eliane Aerts, and Bruce A. B. Cooper, *On Moral Grounds* (New York: New York University Press, 1985), 38.

20. Ibid., 48

21. For a discussion of defense mechanisms see William W. Meissner, "Theories of Personality and Psychopathology: Classical Psychoanalysis," in *Comprehensive Textbook of Psychiatry/IV*, Harold I. Kaplan and Benjamin J. Sadock, eds. (New York: William & Wilkins, 1985), 388–90; Mardi J.

Horowitz, *Introduction to Psychodynamics* (New York: Basic Books, 1988), 191–96; and George E. Valliant, "Theoretical Hierarchy of Adaptive Ego Mechanisms," *Archives of General Psychiatry* 24 (1971): 107–18.

22. For a discussion of emotion see Carroll E. Izard, Jerome Kagan, and Robert B. Zajonc, eds., *Emotions, Cognition and Behavior* (New York: Cambridge, 1984); Nico H. Frijda, "The Law of Emotion," *American Psychologist* 43 (1985): 349–58; and Joseph J. Campos, Rosemary G. Campos, and Karen Caplovitz Barrett, "Emergent Themes in the Study of Emotional Development and Emotion Regulation," *Developmental Psychology* 25 (1989): 394–402.

23. Laurie Denton, "Biosocial Theory Sees Many Roads to Emotion," *APA Monitor* 19 (October 1988): 16.

24. Robert Zajonc, "On the Primacy of Affect," *American Psychologist* 39 (1984): 117–23. For an opposing view see Richard S. Lazarus, "On the Primacy of Cognition," *American Psychologist* 39 (1984): 124–29.

25. David G. Myers, *Psychology* (New York: Worth Publishing, 1986), 388–89.

26. Denton, "Biosocial Theory," 16.

27. Quoted in ibid.

28. Ibid.

29. Kagan, *The Nature of the Child*, 118–19.

30. Ibid.

31. Ibid., 119–20.

32. Robert Emde, William F. Johnson, and M. Ann Easterbrooks, "The Do's and Don't's of Early Moral Development: Psychoanalytic Tradition and Current Research," in *The Emergence of Morality in Young Children*, Jerome Kagan and Sharon Lamb, eds. (Chicago: University of Chicago Press, 1987), 245–76.

33. By "deeply" I mean that at the level of processing, one's affect is experienced as more central (or core) to *who* one is than one's rational beliefs.

34. Robert Jay Lifton, *The Broken Connection* (New York: Simon & Schuster, 1979), 123.

35. Ibid., 123–24.

36. Ibid., 122.

37. Campos et al., "Emergent Themes," 394–99.

38. Lifton, *The Broken Connection*, 122.

39. Ibid., 120–21.

40. Frijda, "The Law of Emotion," 352.

41. Tom Goldstein, "Once Again, 'Billy Budd' Stands Trial," *New York Times*, June 10, 1988.

42. William Braswell, "Melville's *Billy Budd:* An Inside Narrative?" in *Melville's "Billy Budd" and the Critics*, William T. Stafford, ed. (New York: Wadsworth Publishing, 1961), 92.

43. Herman Melville, "Billy Budd, Sailor," *Norton Anthology of American Literature*, vol. 1 (New York: Norton, 1985), 2401.

44. Ibid., 2402.
45. Ibid., 2403.
46. Ibid.
47. Ibid.
48. Braswell, "Melville's *Billy Budd*," 93.
49. Melville, "Billy Budd," 2408.
50. Ibid., 2408.
51. Ibid., 2411.
52. Ibid., 2413.
53. Ibid., 2414.
54. Ibid., 2414–15.
55. Ibid., 2415.
56. Ibid., 2420.
57. E. L. Grant Watson, "Melville's Testament of Acceptance," in *Twentieth Century Interpretations of Billy Budd*, Howard Vincent, ed. (Englewood-Cliffs, N.J.: Prentice-Hall, 1971), 16.
58. William York Tindall, "The Ceremony of Innocence," in *Twentieth Century Interpretations of Billy Budd*, 40.
59. Rahner, " 'Behold This Heart!' " 327.
60. Steven Duffy, "Our Hearts of Darkness: Original Sin Revisited," *Theological Studies* 49 (1988): 597–622.
61. Haan et al., *On Moral Grounds*, 349.
62. Frijda, "The Law of Emotions," 354.
63. Ibid.
64. Ibid.
65. Ibid.
66. Ibid. Frijda's "Law of Hedonic Asymmetry" is a speculative account of how emotions work that is based on his analysis of the research on emotions. My own clinical and pastoral work confirms Frijda's speculation though I will admit the reader might not be persuaded. In any event, I believe that such negative feelings can be overcome through effort thereby fostering our stances as loving men and women.
67. Haan et al., *On Moral Grounds*, 147.
68. Charles M. Shelton, *Morality and the Adolescent* (New York: Crossroad, 1989), 59–109. These pages explore in detail my model of conscience as "other-centered value" and the seven psychological dimensions I believe are necessary for the development of conscience and moral growth.
69. Leonore Fleischer, *Rain Man*, based on a screenplay by Ronald Bass and Barry Morrow and a story by Barry Morrow (New York: New American Library, 1989).
70. Ibid., 13.
71. Ibid., 36.
72. Ibid., 137.
73. Ibid., 189.
74. Ibid., 186.

Chapter 5 — Christian Empathy: The Heart's Vision

1. John L. Elias, *Moral Education Secular and Religious* (Malabar, Fla.: Robert E. Krieger, 1989), vii.

2. Derek Bok, "Ethics, the University, and Society," *Harvard Magazine* 91 (May–June 1988): 39–40.

3. Quoted in Eleanor Smith, "The New Moral Classroom," *Psychology Today* (May 1989): 36.

4. Quoted in Denise K. Magner, "Rash of Ethical Lapses Spurs Colleges to Study Their Moral Responsibilities," *Chronicle of Higher Education* 35 (February 1, 1989): A11.

5. Bok, "Ethics," 47.

6. For a short, concise summary of this issue see Karen J. Winkler, "Scholars Rethink Liberal Theory," *Chronicle of Higher Education* 33 (April 22, 1987): 6–8.

7. Amitai Etzioni, "The 'Me First' Model in the Social Sciences Is Too Narrow," *Chronicle of Higher Education* 35 (February 1, 1989): A44.

8. Robert H. Frank, *Passions within Reason: The Strategic Role of the Emotions* (New York: Norton, 1988).

9. Ibid., 11–12.

10. Ibid., 53.

11. Vartan Gregorian, "'We Need a Moral Center, Not a Moral Enclosure,'" *Chronicle of Higher Education* 35 (May 3, 1989): B5.

12. Ervin Staub, *Positive Social Behavior and Morality*, vol. 1, *Social and Personal Influences* (New York: Academic Press, 1978), 146.

13. Ibid., 148.

14. David M. Stanley, "'Become Imitators of Me': Apostolic Tradition in Paul," in *A Companion to Paul*, Michael J. Taylor, ed. (Staten Island, N.Y.: Alba House, 1975), 211.

15. Edward Schillebeeckx, *Jesus: An Experiment in Christology* (New York: Vintage Books), 665.

16. I do not mean by this explanation of "Christian empathy" to ignore the crucial role of objectivity needed by the pastoral counselor and the boundaries such a role entails. "Christian empathy" would find such a professional role as legitimate. Still, the incorporation of the notion of "Christian empathy" is possible within the pastoral counseling context. The counselor can for example, be concerned about the client, reflect this concern to the client, pray for the client, and act upon situations outside the counseling relationship that might further mental health within the community and abate the problem that led the client to come to counseling (e.g., support community programs that educate the public regarding child abuse).

17. John Donahue, *The Gospel in Parable* (Philadelphia: Fortress Press, 1988), 128–34.

18. Ibid., 131.

19. Ibid., 132.

20. Ibid., 134.

21. For an examination of these Greek words I rely upon the following: Gerhard Kittel, ed., *Theological Dictionary of the New Testament* (Grand Rapids, Mich.: William B. Eerdmans, 1964), 2:477–87; Gerhard Friedrich, ed., *Theological Dictionary of the New Testament* (Grand Rapids, Mich.: William B. Eerdmans, 1971), 7:548–59; Elizabeth R. Achtemeier, "Mercy," in *The Interpreter's Dictionary of the Bible K–Q* (Nashville: Abingdon, 1962), 352–54.

22. Donald P. McNeill, Douglas A. Morrison, Henri J. M. Nouwen, *Compassion* (Garden City, N.J.: Doubleday, 1982), 16.

23. Achtemeier, "Mercy," 353.

24. Kittel, *Dictionary*, 482.

25. Martin L. Hoffman, "Moral Development in Adolescence," in *Handbook of Adolescent Psychology*, Joseph Adelson, ed. (New York: John Wiley, 1980), 306–7.

26. See Augusto Blasi, "Bridging Moral Cognition and Moral Action: A Critical Review of the Literature," *Psychological Bulletin* 88 (1980): 1–41.

27. John M. Darley and C. Daniel Batson, "'From Jerusalem to Jericho': A Study of Situational and Dispositional Variables in Helping Behavior," *Journal of Personality and Social Psychology* 27 (1973): 100–108.

28. Ibid., 107.

29. Anthony G. Greenwald, "Does the Good Samaritan Parable Increase Helping? A Comment on Darley and Batson's No-Effect Conclusion," *Journal of Personality and Social Psychology* 32 (1975): 578–83.

30. St. Ignatius, the founder of the Jesuit Order, wrote the *Spiritual Exercises* as a way to foster spiritual growth in Christian men and women.

31. Quoted in Thomas H. Clancy, *The Conversational Word of God* (St. Louis: Institute of Jesuit Sources, 1978), 26–27.

32. For an excellent critique of competition from a psychological perspective see Morton Deutsch, *Distributive Justice: A Social-Psychological Perspective* (New Haven: Yale University Press, 1985).

33. For a discussion of moral development in adolescence see Hoffman, "Moral Development," 295–343.

34. Kenneth B. Clark, "Empathy: A Neglected Topic in Psychological Research," *American Psychologist* 35 (1980): 189–90.

35. Ibid.

36. Ibid., 190.

Chapter 6 — Living the Heart: Some Pastoral Reflections

1. Jerome Kagan, *The Nature of the Child* (New York: Basic Books, 1984), 124.

2. Bill Puka, "Altruism and Moral Development," in *The Nature of Prosocial Development: Interdisciplinary Theories and Strategies*, Diane L. Bridgeman, ed. (New York: Academic Press, 1983), 197.

3. For a discussion of "consolation" in one's life history see John English, *Choosing Life* (New York: Paulist Press, 1978).

4. The "First Week" of the *Spiritual Exercises* allow one to focus on his or her sinfulness.

5. Nico H. Frijda, "The Laws of Emotion," *American Psychologist* 43 (1988): 354.

6. Fred R. Berger, "Gratitude," in *Vice and Virtue in Everyday Life*, Christina Hoff Sommers, ed. (San Diego: Harcourt Brace Jovanovich, 1985), 198–99.

7. Ibid., 205.

8. Ibid., 206.

9. I do not mean to imply that defense mechanisms can be easily dealt with and acknowledged by an exercise as simple as questioning techniques. Nonetheless, pointed questions that help us to examine our positions and statements serve to aid self-knowledge and self-honesty, which are necessary for sound and healthy moral decisions.

10. Lawrence Hinman, "Emotions, Morality, and Understanding," in *Moral Dilemmas*, Carol Harding, ed. (Chicago: Precedent Publishing, 1985), 68.

Index